TRUE LOVE
AND FORBIDDEN LOVE

AN INVESTIGATION INTO THE CAUSE OF IMMORALITY AND SUFFERING, ITS HISTORICAL ORIGIN AND ITS SOLUTION

Jesus Gonzalez Losada

CUADERNOS PARA LA PAZ

CONTENTS

LIST OF ILLUSTRATIONS

AN INVESTIGATION INTO THE CAUSE OF IMMORALITY AND SUFFERING, ITS HISTORICAL ORIGIN AND ITS SOLUTION

INTRODUCTION

God's eternal and unchanging ideal and man's permanent desire have always been, at the present time and in the course of history, the creation of a unified world of peace, love and happiness for all humanity. However, it is obvious that the reality of this world has been totally different from these ideals which we all fervently desire.

Without clarifying thoroughly the origin of our problems it will be extremely difficult to find the appropriate solutions.

It has always been the greatest challenge for medical science that, before an effective remedy can ever be found and applied, first the real cause of each illness has to be discovered.

Similarly, throughout the course of history, the most difficult task which confronted the founders of the greatest religions, sages, saints, as well as philosophers, was to find the real cause of human suffering and the origin and historical root of evil.

Although many explanations and theories on the origin of evil have been developed, until now no one has been able to clarify this problem satisfactorily and provide an effective solution to end human suffering and tragedy.

The following essay has been inspired by the extraordinary discoveries on this topic made by Rev. Sun Myung Moon, which throw a new light on this yet unresolved, transcendental problem.

The purpose of the author is to familiarize the reader with these important revelations which bring a concrete hope of a new and better future for humanity.

Jesus Gonzalez Losada
New York, July 1992

LOVE AND LIFE

LOVE IS THE SUPREME VALUE

What do we value most in life? What makes us happy? Some will say "money and wealth." Others will respond without doubt: "Wisdom and knowledge." Some others again may suggest: "Power, position and fame." Are money, wealth, knowledge, power and fame then the most important things in our lives?

When we face this question seriously, other thoughts may arise. There is no doubt that we all seek for wealth, knowledge, power and fame which, although valuable, in themselves are not the source of our happiness. Someone could have all the wealth in the world, as well as knowledge but, if obliged to live in isolation, such a person would not be happy. Goals such as money, wealth, knowledge, power and fame only have meaning and value when they are shared or used for the benefit of others.

We are happy when we can share with other people our position, wealth, knowledge or anything of value that we possess. If someone offered you billions of dollars as well as knowledge and power in exchange for your loving spouse, parents or children, would you sell them? Would you be happy afterwards? Only when we have harmonious relationships of true love with others can we experience the greatest happiness.

Consequently, happiness requires a relationship with someone and this is true as much for God as for man. Therefore, we have to come to the conclusion that what is most precious in life is love. No amount of money, power or knowledge can ever match the infinite power of true love. It does not matter how long we live: our biological existence does not have value unless we experience love.

When we observe our universe, we realize that each being exists through the union of a pair of elements. That is true on all levels, starting even from the mineral kingdom. Atoms and molecules are formed by the union of a positive and negative element. In plants, existence and reproduction requires the union of stamen and pistil, which represent the masculine and feminine aspects.

The system of pairs is even more obvious in the animal kingdom. Fish, birds, mammals and other animals exist as male and female and human beings exist as men and women.

Why does this system of pairs exist? Was there ever, throughout history, any man who planned to create himself and his descendants as masculine, with all his organs and characteristics, and a feminine complement, to form a home and procreate? Did any woman plan it? Of course not. Who did so? It is reasonable to admit that it would have to be the original Creator, the first to think, plan and design, who created us as man and woman for the purpose of consummating a union in love.

The Creator divided all things into masculine and feminine so that they could unite and multiply through the giving and receiving of love. God created everything with a reciprocal partner so that all levels of creation would experience joy and love. Through the action of love, each species multiplies and extends its lineage.

The concept of love was first in God's mind and only afterwards did He create man and woman. Man and woman could only find true love through each other.

Do we men and women live for the purpose of eating three times a day and sleeping eight hours every night? Certainly not. We live for the ecstasy and the fulfillment of love. This is the way God created us.

God is the first personality and the human personality originates from God. This is why men and women are willing to sacrifice their own lives for the benefit of the ones they love.

The word "sacred" should be connected to love; only in the context of love has the word "sacred" any meaning. For example, any husband who is capable of sacrificing for the well-being of his wife is a sacred husband, and vice versa. A person who is willing to die for his or her parents is a child of filial piety, a sacred son or daughter. The person who gives his or her life for the well-being or benefit of humanity is a saint.

Love is the supreme value. Love does not exist for myself, but for others. True love begins when we sacrifice ourselves and live for the purpose of loving others. True love is altruistic or unselfish, giving constantly for the benefit of others, forgetting all that was given. If you consciously remember what you have given, then you will begin to calculate how much giving is enough. And if you decide that you have given enough, then love cannot continue eternally. True love is the act of giving without the condition of receiving.

We should all surrender before this true love. True love has power and domain over everything, only true love transcends all barriers. To call something true, it should contain four characteristics: it should be unique, eternal, unchanging and absolute.

LOVE AND THE PURPOSE OF LIFE

God's eternal and unchanging ideal is the creation of a world of love, peace and happiness for all humanity. "Heart" is the most important and at the core of all the attributes that exist in the Divine character. We could define "heart" as the emotional impulse to experience happiness through love. In the heart of God there is an unrestrained emotional force and desire to love. This is the reason why religious people say that God is love, because love originates in God. (I John 4:7-8)

Love can only exist when we love someone or someone loves us. God needed to create humanity to communicate His love. It is for the sake of love that human beings are the supreme creation.

An ideal needs to be shared with someone. This was the profound reason which motivated God to create mankind, whom He created in His image and likeness as the visible manifestation of His invisible characteristics, as objects of His love, in the position of His children, to be the source of His happiness and to share His creativity.

God created the physical and the spiritual world as the environment and object of enjoyment for humanity. If we were able to become one with God in true love, we could have dominion over God's creation, both the physical as well as the spiritual world.

True love contains the three great attributes of "inheritance," "participation," and "equality." For example, if a poor woman who did not have the means to get an education is married to the president, and they are a loving couple, then what belongs to the husband belongs to the wife. She has the right to participate in her husband's interests and because they love each other more than themselves they are equal in value.

When we live our lives completely for others, we reach gradually the same essence and characteristics of God. The vibrations of God are converted in our vibrations and God's feelings are transmitted to us naturally. Living in this manner, we become a resonant body of God's heart and love. This is the state of perfection which God wants us to reach and it is for that purpose that He originally created us.

In order to carry out such purpose, God created man and woman so that they could first grow and reach their individual maturity and perfection. Ultimately, with His blessing they would unite intoxicated in love, establishing an eternal couple and becoming True Parents for their children, transmitting to them physical and spiritual life. (This ideal is expressed in Genesis 1:28).

The purpose of our existence is to realize this ideal of true love and happiness in the family, which will naturally extend outward into the society, nation and world.
From all the existing institutions or many others that can be created, the family is the first and most important, having God as its very founder. The family is the fundamental unit and the indispensably building block of any society. If we cannot establish peace, love and happiness in our homes, there will be no hope of creating peace, love and happiness in the larger world. Good families are the basis for a healthy, prosperous and happy society anywhere. (See diagram #1).

THE BASIS FOR A HEALTHY AND

HAPPY SOCIETY

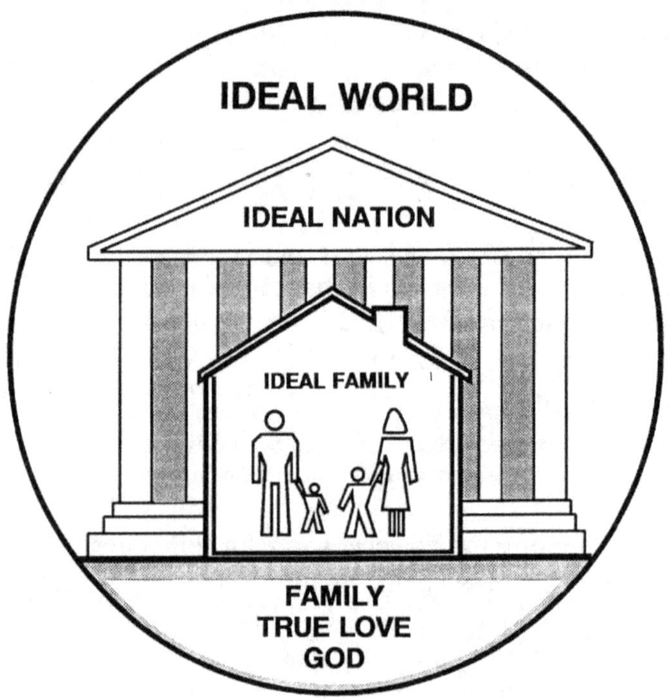

The family is the fundamental unit of society. If we cannot establish the ideal in our homes, there will be no hope of creating an ideal society, nation or ideal world. The family is the school of love and the ideal place where the love of God is seen expressed in human relationships.

DIAGRAM 1

The family is the school of love and the ideal place where the love of God is seen expressed in human relationships. In the family, one is to grow to experience and learn the widening realms of love: initially children's love towards one's parents, then love among one's brothers and sisters, then conjugal love with one's spouse, and, finally, parental love towards one's own children. When we learn and practice this four realms of heart we can graduate from this school of love. Through this process we become prepare to master all human relationships in the larger society.

When we look at a family, we see that parents stand in the center. The family could only be formed because of the love between a man and a woman. Love is like the glue, the very element that brings them together and also maintains continuing unity. The love of parents is the origin of our physical and spiritual life and transmits the blood lineage. Therefore it is crucial to talk about the value and purpose of love in human life.

Throughout history, numerous viewpoints addressing life, the universe and God have presented unresolved problems. The solution to those problems will be found when a true man and a true woman unite with God in true love, creating an absolute unit, due to the fact that this is God's original purpose and the source of absolute value.

If we observe adolescents, we can see that they are preparing themselves physically and spiritually for the experience of love. They are usually very romantic, idealistic, sensitive and passionate. These are the signs that they are opening themselves to the complete sensation of love, in body, mind and spirit. They are like a blossom before opening. The sweetness is kept inside. Therefore, before they can be blessed in marriage they should be like a bud, very closed, keeping in this way the fragrance and sweetness in the core of their being. Each young person should value and carefully keep his or her chastity and purity as the most valuable treasure. This is the best guarantee for the success of their future family. Chastity and purity of heart before marriage allow for the continuing growth of one's personality and spirit. There is a definite correlation between one's development of a healthy sexuality and one's spiritual growth towards a virtuous adulthood. All this elements are needed in order to successfully build a bond of true and lasting love in marriage. On that foundation, man and woman can establish a strong couple and become good parents for their children, transmitting to them a true tradition of love to follow. This is the divine principle.

God created man for the sake of woman and woman for the sake of man. So we can say that from the moment a person is born he or she was born for his or her mate. Man and woman are the substantial manifestations of the masculine and feminine characteristics which come from God. They are like energy accumulators, loading energy originating from God, but of an opposite polarity. It is as if some kind of electricity is generated between man and woman, such as between the positive and negative pole of an electric circuit which, once connected, causes electricity to flow; God would generate more and more voltage between them, creating an enormous spark and explosion like a fireball of love. That spark means unity and creativity.

When love is produced between a man and a woman, a kind of magnetic field is generated flowing from God. Therefore, all creation is like a love machine. God created human beings to be the internal part of the machine, while the universe is the external part. Both parts vibrate, united with the same wavelength of love.

Where are man and woman finally connected for the consummation of their love? Through their sexual organs. The man's organs of love, as well as the woman's, are located in the center of the body, where all the nervous systems are concentrated. God put them in a protected place, like a hidden construction.

These organs, if man had not been degraded in the beginning, should in the last instance be connected to their center of energy, which is God. The sexual organs should originally be the palaces of God's love. They were supposed to be the most important and sacred places, through which love is consummated, life created and lineage transmitted.

The sexual union in marriage should have a sacred and mystic dimension, because the God-centered intimate sexual union of a husband and wife allows them to experience the love that God originally designed.

God created men and women in such a way that they harmonize sexually. The man's sexual organ is owned by his wife and vice versa. This is the simple truth and no power can change this truth. They exchange ownership and then there is only one owner forever; it is as if each partner voluntarily puts on a chastity belt and confides the key to the other spouse. Problems have arisen through the idea that we have ownership over our sexual organ and we have the right to use it in accord with whatever our body dictates.

We need to consider a fundamental principle in the pursuit of a happy and stable family: **that sex belongs only to marriage.** Only husband and wife have the access key in order to open those sacred places for the consummation of heavenly love. The act of love is meant to be a husband and wife's most holy possession and should never be defiled by allowing a stranger to enter and corrupt it. This is the only correct way to understand the relationship between husband and wife. Once a man and a woman find their true love, it is something permanent and eternal and an alternative love could not exist.

The first night when the sharing of the first love, the moment when husband and wife join together in total unity through a complete physical and spiritual love, when the sexual organs join in total harmony -that is the point where the whole purpose of creation is fulfilled.

God gave men and women sexual organs so they could join together, which is the most incredible blessing. Through their coming together, God wants to feel joy in the True Love palace. This is the beginning point of true happiness.

We inherit our blood lineage through the sexual act. That is not only the consummation point for men and women, it is also the point of consummation for God. The entire invisible image of God is completed upon this point. The spiritual world and the physical world, creator and created, all become one at that point. This is where the joy of creation comes into being. This is the beginning of happiness and hope and we must restore this, we must attain this. This is the life which God envisioned for every man and woman here on earth and when you finish this kind of earthly life, you will go to the Kingdom of Heaven in the eternal spiritual world.

Men and women's definite stimulus and realization are those of true love; nothing better exists. It is like the anchor of life. When a husband and wife's love consummate at this sacred level, God is living with them at every moment.

Once anchored in the heart of God, husband and wife could feel totally satisfied and fulfilled forever.

The love of our parents is the origin of our physical and spiritual life and transmits the blood lineage. Love, life and lineage are connected with the sexual organs. The linkage of love, life and lineage is what gives history its continuity, connecting the past, the present and the future.

That is why the act of love should be the most precious, beautiful and sacred act of our life. But, in spite of that, it is very shocking to discover that constantly throughout human history, the sexual organs and the act of love have been seen as something dirty and shameful. It is also symptomatic that most languages frequently use the most obscene and vulgar words to describe the sexual organs and the act of love.

Although adultery is the biggest imaginable betrayal against true love, we nevertheless see this problem unfortunately repeated in all types of environments and cultures through the ages, as well as the fact that prostitution degrades sex to a mere commodity. Incest, abortion, rape and all sexual perversions are carried out through these love organs, that had tainted human life in all races and cultures throughout human history. These are clear reasons which prove that something terribly abnormal and wrong exists in human conduct in relation to love and its sexual expression. It also reveals to us, as we will see later on, that human beings deviated in their origin and were degraded by taking a false direction in matters of love.

The sexual impulse is the most powerful inner force. If we are not able to control, conquer and use it in the correct direction, then this sexual drive will be the very force that will conquer, dominate and eventually destroy us. This is the reason why it has been so difficult for people to overcome the desire for illicit love. All the greatest religions in history have dealt with overcoming this particular problem and this is why they all acknowledged adultery and fornication as the worst sin. In many cases, a life of celibacy was even promoted and encouraged as the means of purification and attaining the highest dimension of the love of God. In this manner, a clear distinction is drawn between the divine, heavenly and original love that they desire to reach and the degraded and corrupt level of the worldly love which we see around us.

Love is the greatest and most powerful force in the universe and the source of life and happiness. The act of love is destined to be, according to the divine principle, the most beautiful, sacred and sublime experience. But if this act is carried out in an illicit way it becomes the dirtiest, most degraded and shameful experience. Therefore, illicit or forbidden love is also a very destructive force that causes enormous frustrations, disappointments and suffering.

An analogy can be made between the physical power of atomic energy and the spiritual power of love. If atomic energy is used wisely for peaceful purposes, it can allow for unimaginable prosperity and progress. But if it is wrongly used, atomic power can cause unimaginable destruction and death. In the same way, love experienced in a constructive direction gives us the greatest happiness, but when experienced in an immature or improper way it can result in divorce, unwanted pregnancies, abortions, incest, domestic violence, etc.

(See diagram # 2).

SUFFERING ORIGINATES IN THE WRONG USE OF LOVE

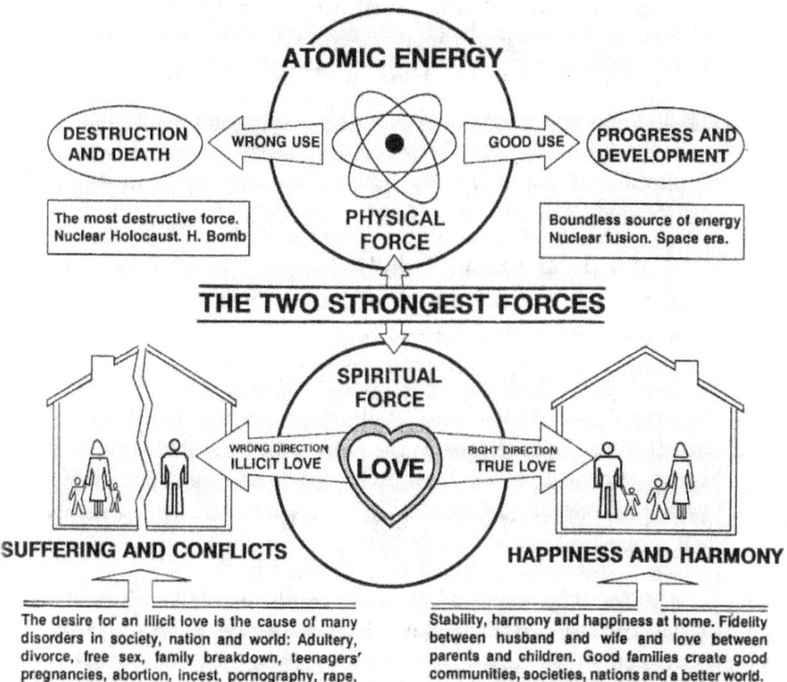

The desire for an illicit love is the cause of many disorders in society, nation and world: Adultery, divorce, free sex, family breakdown, teenagers' pregnancies, abortion, incest, pornography, rape, prostitution, homosexuality, sexual perversions... HELL is the state of suffering that starts with the misuse and abuse of love.

Stability, harmony and happiness at home. Fidelity between husband and wife and love between parents and children. Good families create good communities, societies, nations and a better world. The KINGDOM OF HEAVEN is the religious expression referring to the kingdom of true love and eternal happiness.

Love is the greatest and most powerful force in the universe and the source of life and happiness

The act of love is destined to be, according to the divine principle, the most beautiful, sacred and sublime experience. But, if this act is carried out in an illicit way it becomes the dirtiest, most degraded and shameful experience. Therefore, illicit or forbidden love is also a very destructive force that causes enormous frustrations, disappointments and suffering.

DIAGRAM 2

THE TRAGIC RESULTS OF THE WRONG USE OF LOVE

Sexual corruption has caused the fall of important and famous people, nations and empires throughout human history. As the main enemy of the family, illicit love bears tragic consequences for individuals, families, and for the society as well.

The previous statement contains a very ancient and implacable wisdom. From the very early times, sages, prophets and people shared the belief that sooner or later uncontrolled sexual conduct would be a serious offense against the gods and would bring misfortune in the form of decadence and self-destruction. In the Bible it is written that the cities of Sodom and Gomorrah were destroyed because the people who lived there led a very immoral life.

Modern investigations corroborate this belief. Arnold Toynbee, one of the most prominent modern historians, writes: "Out of twenty-one of the most notable civilizations in history, nineteen perished not by having been conquered, but because of internal decadence."

Another historian, Dr. J.D. Unwin from Cambridge University, who made a study of eighty civilizations that existed over a period of four thousand years, came to the conclusion that those civilizations who chose sexual promiscuity degenerated, but those who exercised sexual discipline created prosperity. Sigmund Freud, the founder of psychoanalysis, expressed: "I could say over and over again - because I was never able to prove otherwise - that sexuality is the key to disclose the problem of psychoneurosis and neurosis in general." (Three Essays on the Theory of Sexuality).

The Roman Empire managed to become incredibly strong and powerful in its time but eventually collapsed, not because of a formidable invading external army, but due to internal decadence that made it weak and vulnerable. From the emperors to the common people, many indulged in a hedonistic and lustful life. When archaeologists discovered the ruins of the city of Pompeii in Italy, which was caught by surprise and buried by the eruption of Mt. Vesuvius, they were able to reconstruct scenes of the life at the moment of the eruption which corroborated that the life style of its inhabitants was lustful, licentious and immoral.

In the light of what has been expressed previously, the idea that sex is no more then a simple biological necessity, an appetite that one must satisfy, like drinking "a glass of water" when one is thirsty, is totally mistaken. And it is sustained by the erroneous understanding of many that man is just an evolved and rational animal, which is trying to completely negate man's spiritual and divine dimension.

We need to eat, drink, sleep, have clothes and shelter for our individual survival. Sexual activity is necessary from the biological point of view for the procreation of our species, but not in order to maintain our individual physical existence. The sexual act is not merely a physical function, sex is interpersonal and affects another person directly. As we have already seen, its true purpose is bound to be the inseparable expression of true love.

If we have any doubts about this, we should check what happened in Russia during the first years of the revolution. In the beginning deliberate attacks were made against marriage and the family. Divorce could be obtained for any reason and at any moment. Abortion was legal and facilitated. Premarital relationships were favored. Sexual relationships outside marriage were viewed as normal.

What happened? According to Professor Sorokin of Harvard University, after a few years hordes of savage boys and girls without a home were a real threat to the country. Millions of lives, especially girls', were destroyed and divorce and abortion reached unheard of limits. Hatred and conflicts produced by the polygamy and polyandry increased rapidly, as did psychoneurosis. Work at the nationalized factories was neglected.

The results were so alarming that the government was obliged to reverse its policies. The propaganda of the "glass of water" was declared contrary to the revolution and in its place an official glorification of chastity and of the sanctity of marriage was installed.

In other words, the Russians discovered the reality that sex, regarded as an appetite, ruined not only the individual but also rapidly the state itself.

Harmony and social stability begin, naturally, with the harmony and stability at home. It is a very common observation that the family is the moral foundation of society, therefore the ethical and moral standard of a nation is a reflection of the moral standard of its families.

We need affection and love for our internal growth just as we need physical nourishment for our body. When a youngster does not receive adequate nourishment when growing up, the body will suffer rickets, malnutrition and other problems which will affect its formation.

The same occurs when we do not receive love, attention and the necessary care and affection from our parents at home: it results in limitations, complexities and other problems which eventually affect our character and adult behavior.

Numerous statistical and sociological investigations demonstrate that many delinquents and criminals come from disintegrated homes and that most of the problems of alcoholism, drug addiction and violence are linked to the distortion or lack of love received at home. Indeed, where there is homosexuality, free sex, drugs, and alcoholism, the world of true love is far away. How many have been touched by the cruelty of infidelity and divorce? Where is God in all the one-night stands? What about the nightmare of the children who are sexually abused by a parent? Is free sex worth the price of a broken child? Free sex is what pains God the most. A world of free sex is absolutely contrary to the will of God and the ideal of the family. Love comes from the stimulation of unblemished emotion, but free sex is totally devoid of purity or true emotion.

At the present time, many problems can gradually be solved by the advance of science, technology and the employment of new and more advanced political, social and economic systems. But, despite the magnitude of these advances, it seems that the more a country develops the less capable it is of recognizing and controlling sexual immorality, adultery and all the sexually related crimes.

Such acts are normally being carried out in privacy and secrecy. This is a problem that neither laws, pills, technology, nor the current contemporary methods of sexual education, are capable of resolving.

Unfortunately, many of the modern programs of sexual education for the young present purely physical (genital) information, focusing only on the biological, medical and hygienic aspects of sex, with a range of details about all kinds of possible methods and devices to avoid pregnancy and sexually transmitted diseases. This teaching is devoid of ethical and moral values, and pitifully fails to acknowledge the true and sacred purpose of love and its sexual expression, Not surprisingly, the result of this type of education has been to **increase** the very problems it claims to avoid!

Instead of emphasizing the value of chastity and a serious preparation for true love and marriage, these methods have served in many cases as an open invitation to a premature sexual experiences, spreading the attitude that sex is a mere biological necessity and that the repercussions only constitute a problem if the appropriate measures are not taken.

THE NECESSITY OF ANSWERS AND SOLUTIONS

As we have just discussed, love should be focused according to the divine plan or principle, in a correct and true direction, producing good results and, without doubt, be the source of happiness and the fulfillment of our ideals.

But unfortunately, as we have already explained, all throughout history people have not known how to find the true direction in relation to love and reach the ideals that we so earnestly desire.

When and how did this tendency of choosing a false and illicit direction in love originate? What is the cause of this deviation? If God is our creator and His eternal and unchanging ideal is the realization of a unified world of love, peace and happiness, why is this world a place of suffering and tragedy so different from the divine ideal?

Up to now nobody has been able to clarify satisfactorily with depth and detail all those questions and offer really effective solutions to end human suffering and tragedy.

From all the investigations ever made, the one we are about to present is the most important one. From all the secrets ever revealed this is also the most transcendental.

The extraordinary discoveries made by Rev. Sun Myung Moon on this topic have an immeasurable value and represent an essential contribution clarifying this problem which was never before resolved satisfactorily.

Sun Myung Moon began a long and arduous pursuit in search of these hidden secrets and mysteries on Easter morning April 17, 1935 on a mountainside in the Northwest of the Korean peninsula, his native country.

At the age of 15, while in deep prayer and extremely distressed by the suffering that he observed around him that, lamentably, was a continuation of the human experience throughout history, Jesus Christ appeared to him in a vision and showed him the course of events of his life.

Due to the ignorance and intolerance of his contemporaries, Jesus' life was filled with suffering and pain. In spite of all the preparation of Israel carried out by God, including the sending of prophets and giving signs before the arrival of the Messiah, Jesus was faced with denial and opposition in his time, because the people could neither recognize nor accept his true role and position as the Messiah. This failure of the chosen people to unite with the awaited Messiah led them to consider him an impostor and ultimately crucify him after only three years of Jesus' public ministry. Nevertheless, Jesus always maintained a heart of unconditional love and was victorious in bringing spiritual salvation to humanity through his example and sacrifice on the cross.

However, the immense hope and expectations of God and Jesus to finally eradicate sin from the face of the earth at that time, and physically establish the Kingdom of Heaven, were not completed. This hope still remains unfulfilled.

Jesus explained to the young Moon the necessity that someone should seriously carry on the task of completing this mission and he asked him to accept that responsibility.

In spite of his age, Sun Myung Moon had already felt the tragedy and suffering of humanity, and was determined to dedicate his life to remedy it. But this revelation occurred suddenly and he was very astonished. He was asked to make an extremely difficult and important decision.

In the beginning he rejected the mission, but finally he accepted. As he would explain years later to his followers, he did it for two reasons: Firstly, if he had not accepted, Jesus might not have found anyone else. Secondly, if he began such a task by his own determination, he would always have had the option of abandoning it in the future, but if a solemn pledge was made to someone, in this case to Jesus Christ, then he would have to persevere until the end.

After this profound and overwhelming experience, everything completely changed in his life and during the following nine years he undertook an intense search for the truth.

Although outwardly he continued his studies, graduating in electric engineering, all his free time was dedicated to prayer, study of the Bible and other sacred books. He was intense, serious and concerned, preparing for his mission. He wandered in the mountains and along the rivers, meditating, fasting, praying, investigating.

The answers never came in an easy way. He had to fight intense and fierce spiritual battles with evil satanic forces which wanted to block his search for the truth which could liberate humanity from sin and suffering.

Through innumerable nights spent in prayer, he experienced profound spiritual communication with Jesus Christ, Moses, Buddha and other saints, as well as direct communication with God.

He fought desperately in order to solve the huge spiritual enigma of such questions as:

Who is God? What is His nature? What is His intention and purpose? Why did He create man? What is the relationship that must exist between human beings and their Creator? This was one of the answers which God Himself revealed directly to him:

"The basic and central truth of this universe is that God is our Father and we are his children. All people were created as God's children."

Consequently, he asked Heavenly Father: Why do not we enjoy this intimate relationship like Father and son with you now? By which means, process, reason, when and by whom was this relationship destroyed? By Satan? Who is Satan? Who created Satan? Why did Satan become Satan? If You are good and the only Creator, how could evil appear? If nobody created Satan, how did Satan come to exist?

If God is love and taught us to forgive our enemy 70 times 7, why could not this very God forgive Satan? Why? ... What kind of conceivable deed could Satan have done, that is impossible even for God to forgive? What kind of sin was committed in the beginning, that brought so much tragedy to this world? What exactly was the so-called original sin? Why did it affect us and continues to affect us so deeply?

If God is almighty, how could God permit the existence of evil? Why does God seem incapable, impotent? Why?.. Who is responsible to solve the problem of evil? God? Man? The Messiah?

God and Jesus had been waiting for someone who could finally proclaim to the world Satan's identity and his hidden crime, so that he could be accused and judged in front of God.

To be able to clarify and expose the nature of the original sin, was the most complex and formidable task.

Once Sun Myung Moon discovered the unbearable betrayal committed against God and His ideal of love in the beginning of human history, the knowledge of this secret was the best weapon to defend himself and counterattack the forces of evil, and the key that enabled him to discover the path along which mankind has to travel in order to be restored to the originally intended state of goodness and perfection. He discovered not only that part of the path we have already covered for some distance in the past, but also the part we still have to complete in the future.

At that time, Sun Myung Moon began to understand intensely the anguished heart of our Heavenly Father, who constantly suffered and still continues to suffer because of the tribulations and sins of all his children. Although many people abandoned God, He never abandoned anyone. In spite of his loneliness and sorrow, He constantly worked for the salvation of humanity.

Realizing and feeling this tragedy Sun Myung Moon cried endlessly upon discovering Heavenly Father's miserable situation. Sometimes his clothes were completely soaked by his tears and his face so swollen that even his neighbors could not recognize him.

He continued to ask: Through which principles have You been working throughout human history in order to restore humanity? Why was the Kingdom of Heaven that Jesus Christ proclaimed, not established when he was here on earth? What were the circumstances and the reasons why Jesus was rejected and crucified two thousand years ago? When will the end of the world, announced in the Bible, take place? Why does the world have to come to an end?

How does the world end? Will it be a catastrophe of the universe, or not? If not, what is the real meaning of the unusual phenomena predicted in the Bible? How and when will evil and sin finally be eradicated from human history? After many incredible ordeals, Sun Myung Moon was finally victorious and received answers to these and many other questions, which were later systematically written down by his followers in what we know today as the *Divine Principle*.

Rev. Moon commented in 1972 in London: *"I am revealing a topic of the biggest controversy in the contemporary theological world. Its content is not merely a study or investigation of the Bible. It is a revelation that came after an intense search and exploration in the most remote places of the spiritual world, where I received the answers. Therefore, my most serious desire is that you do not rush in making prejudgments. Please, hold your conclusions until you make your own investigations, particularly in the spiritual world.*
I know clearly that God's law is very severe. If I proclaim something which is not true, then I know that I will receive the judgement of history. I have suffered persecution all my life only because I am speaking the truth and for that reason only. There are two ways of checking this. We can verify it here on earth or we can confirm this truth in the spiritual world. I say this to you because I hope that you will meditate deeply about this and consider it seriously."

Next we are going to expose some concepts that will help us to understand much better these revelations about the historical origin of evil and its implications in what is traditionally known as **"the fall of man"**.

WHEN, HOW AND WHY DID EVIL, SUFFERING AND THE HUMAN TRAGEDY BEGIN?

Throughout all recorded human history we notice the existence of an unnatural evil nature in man, which caused conflicts and contradictions and brought much suffering and tragedy in our lives. As anthropologist Richard Heinberg has stated: "People of every culture and age have insisted that evil had a specific cause..., that human nature is not natural at all because it has been distorted by some fundamental mistake or failure that has perpetuated itself from generation to generation." (Memories and Visions of Paradise)

It is therefore reasonable to assume that evil appeared at the very beginning of our existence on this planet, starting most probably from our original ancestors.

As this is a problem that goes beyond the reach of science, we must try to understand it from a religious perspective.

It is very revealing and significant when we discover the fact that almost all cultures and religions in the world teach some kind of myth or legend about what happened at the dawn of history, recognizing that mankind lost its original direction and at a certain point became corrupted and evil.

In Egyptian stories, for example, there are references to a lost golden age and death caused by the "female ancestor" and the serpent. Indian legends reveal to us that Brahma was tempted by Shiva to make him believe that the flower of the tree of knowledge would give him immortality.

In the Greek mythology, Pandora's box is a famous example. Pandora was a woman who was going to marry one of the gods, before the existence of evil. They gave her a box and asked her not to open it until the wedding night was over. However, she could not resist or control her curiosity and upon opening it terrible misfortunes and calamities befell the human race. The Bible tells the story of Adam and Eve.

The famous psychoanalyst, Carl Jung, understood these stories not merely as superstition or myth, but as important revelations of a truth far beyond the comprehension of our rational mind. For Jung, these were symbolic expressions of the collective memory of the human race, a treasure of secrets coming from our subconscious collective mind that tells us about our past as human beings.

Out of all the stories dealing with what religions traditionally call "the human fall", the Bible contains the most detailed account and the one which has caused the biggest impact on the different world cultural spheres. Consequently, this story deserves our undivided attention.

The book of Genesis in the Bible describes to us that the first man (Adam) and the first woman (Eve) lived in the "Garden of Eden", a world of happiness, without fear, shame or evil. This garden had two trees in its center. God gave full freedom to Adam and Eve, but commanded them not to eat the "fruit" of the "Tree of the Knowledge of Good and Evil", with a serious warning that if they ate it they would die.

Tempted by a "serpent", the woman ate of the forbidden fruit and then shared it with the man. As a result, both felt afterwards ashamed of their nakedness and hid themselves from God. Next, God cursed the serpent and expelled Adam and Eve from the Garden and placed an angel at its entrance to keep man from reaching the "Tree of Life", the other tree standing in the center of the garden.

This was the fall of our original ancestors in accordance with the biblical narrative.

Let's scrutinize this story in detail in order to decipher its various symbols, enabling us to understand its meaning and message relative to mankind's present situation.

THE SEARCH FOR OUR FIRST ANCESTORS

One of the characteristics distinguishing human beings from other animals is the possession of a unique, eternal and indestructible spirit. Therefore when we mention the first original couple [according to the Bible, "Adam and Eve"] we refer to the first masculine, eternal and indestructible spirit of a man [Adam] and of a woman [Eve]. Both represent and embody God's masculine and feminine characteristics, and were supposed to become the visible manifestation of His invisible characteristics [image and likeness]. These first incarnate human spirits were created to be God's children and lords and heirs of all creation. The rest of all existent human spirits originated from these two first [father and mother] human spirits.

Our fundamental concern is to clarify their spiritual and divine origin as well as the purpose for their creation, and not so much the details of their biological or physical origin. The question of physical origin falls in to the field of science which, hopefully, will give an answer some time in the future. Even under the assumption that multiple humanoids were involved in our biological origin it would not present a problem with the basic view of the *Divine Principle*. Nevertheless, there are very interesting new discoveries about our origins recently done through genetic biology:

Modern biologists Rebecca L. Cann, Mark Stoneking and Allan C. Wilson of California University, Berkeley, made an investigation of tracing the genetic code of the mitochondrial DNA contained in our cells, which they extracted from 147 placentas from women of all races and geographical areas on the five continents. Curiously enough, the mitochondrial DNA is inherited and transmitted exclusively by our mothers. The results of this study brought a powerful and revealing conclusion: each one of us, as part of the human race, can trace our lineage back to one single woman, nicknamed "Mitochondrial Eve" by these scientists.

These results were published on January 1, 1987 under the title: *"Mitochondrial DNA and Human Evolution"* in NATURE, one of the more prestigious scientific magazines.
This investigation caused a huge controversy and later many attempts were made to discredit its conclusions. Although these attempts were successful in undermining the claims of race, time and place of the appearance of this supposed "first woman," the fundamental assumption that our genes come from "her" still remain unchallenged.

More recently, in a study published in the journal of Science (26-5-95) scientists Robert L. Dorit (Yale University), Walter Gilbert (Harvard University) and Hiroshi Akashi (university of Chicago) have dealt a blow to the idea that modern humans arose simultaneously in different parts of the world. Analyzing a gene on the Y chromosome of 38 men from all over the glove, they found no variation -and thus conclude that humanity's ancestors formed a small, concentrated population. The findings are consistent with the prevalent view among anthropologists that the origin of the species was a recent event that happened in one region and that humans then spread over the world. Today's racial variations would have arisen after that dispersal.

The human race began at a certain specific point in the history of our planet, just as our own individual physical life also had a precise beginning. Consequently it is reasonable to make the following comparison:

Our father and mother are the beginning point of our life. They transmitted to us their characteristics and genes, contained in the two original cells that united at the moment of conception, which after continuously multiplying resulted in the massive quantity of cells that formed the organs of our body. Each cell in our body carries an exclusive genetic code, characteristic of each individual, which originated from the two original cells.

In a very similar way, the more than 5,500 million people which now form the worldwide population, originated from the multiplication that occurred through all the different generations which existed over time, and eventually, upon moving backwards in our genealogical tree, would bring us to our original ancestors. The first father and first mother, the first human couple, the starting point of our species. Each one of us carries this exclusive genetic code and characteristic of our species, given by these original parents.

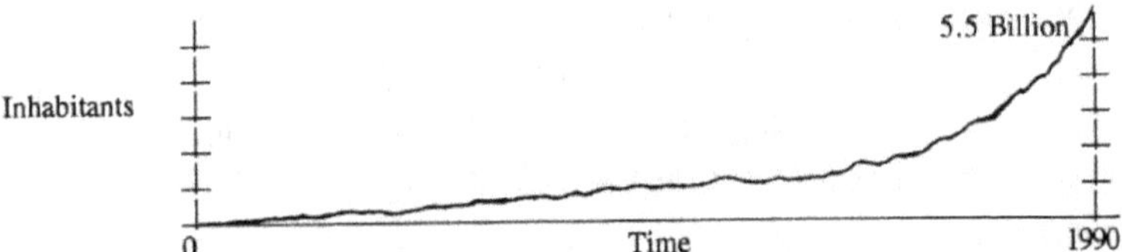

[Each individual without exception originates from a father and a mother. It is therefore a mathematical problem of statistics of the population growth to regress from the approximately 5,500,000,000 present inhabitants of the word population until the time of zero inhabitants and obviously the next number after the zero that we can mathematically consider should be necessarily number 2, as 1 or 1.5 in this case cannot procreate.]

Will biologists ultimately reach the conclusion that, the Adam and Eve of the biblical story, the first couple and our human ancestors, did in fact actually exist?

We have to be grateful that today several findings in contemporary science are helping us to unify and clarify many of these ancient religious beliefs. Especially, the new and revolutionary discoveries in the areas of quantum physics, molecular biology and parapsychology.

Unfortunately in past centuries, from the time of Galileo Galilei, serious and irreconcilable disputes arose between the religious and scientific viewpoints, basically provoked by ignorance and fanaticism, which were many times present on both sides. According to the *Divine Principle*, contradictions between science and religion should not exist. As Rev. Moon humorously expressed to a group of scientists who were interested to know why a religious leader sponsored huge conferences for scientists, he replied: "God is the oldest and number one scientist." Science and religion should work together and in harmony, since both serve to overcome our external and internal ignorance. As Albert Einstein put it: "Science without religion is crippled and religion without science is blind."

THE MEANING OF THE SYMBOLS

THE GARDEN OF EDEN: The Hebrew word for "eden" means happiness or delight, which indicates to us that human beings were supposed to live in joy and happiness. The "Garden of Eden" represents, therefore, this Ideal World or Earthly Paradise, that would be accomplished upon the completion of what the *Divine Principle* calls "the three great blessings":

<u>The first blessing</u>: refers to the fulfillment of our individual perfection.

<u>The second blessing</u>: refers to the establishment of a true family of eternal love.

<u>The third blessing</u>: refers to the harmony and unity between the human family and the whole creation (as caretakers and protectors of the environment).

These gifts or divine blessings should be the essential goals to be accomplished by every person and we find them expressed in verse 1:28 of Genesis : "...be fruitful and multiply and fill the earth and subdue it..."

(see diagram #3).

THE REALIZATION OF THE PURPOSE OF OUR LIFE

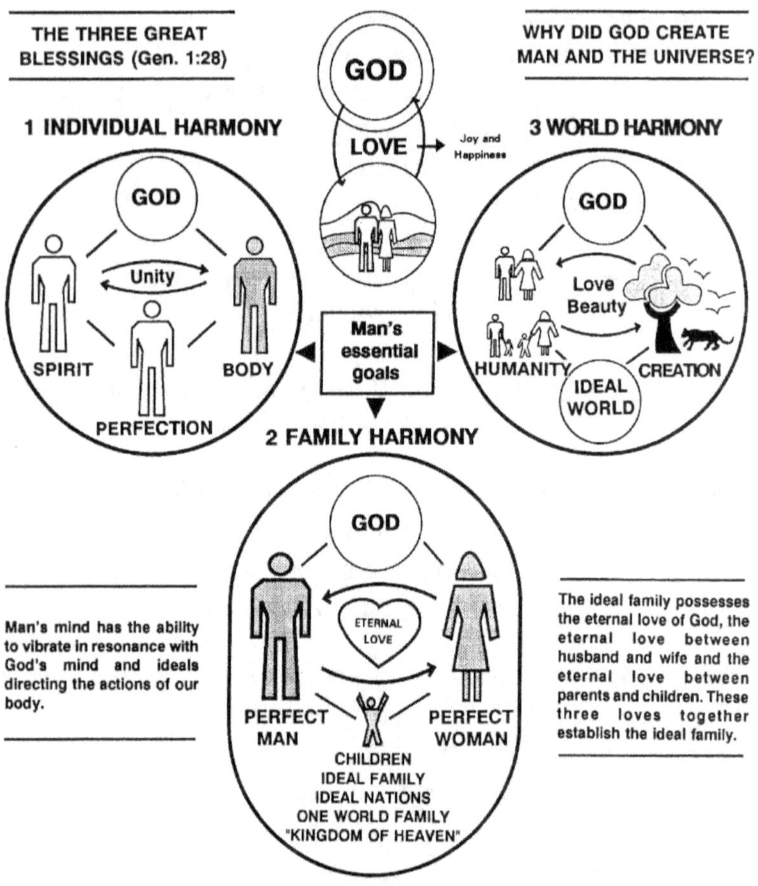

DIAGRAM 3

Adam and Eve were supposed to grow and reach physical as well as spiritual maturity as God's son and daughter, in other words, become one with God in heart, love and ideals.

In this way, Adam and Eve were meant to be the incarnation or the visible manifestation of the invisible God. The temple where the Spirit of God would dwell constantly.

Then, with God's permission and blessing, they should have united intoxicated with a heavenly love, establish an eternal couple and become the True Parents of mankind who could transmit physical and spiritual life to their children. They were destined to establish the tradition of true love and eternal happiness that should be followed by all their descendants and eventually all humanity.

This realm of true love and eternal happiness was supposed to continue expanding into the spiritual dimension or Spirit World after the death of our physical body. Through the human family, God would have exercised a dominion of love over the whole creation both in this physical universe and in the spiritual world.

All of this would be a reality today if human beings would not have been degraded by sin in the very beginning. For this reason, man's permanent desire is to recuperate and restore that lost Garden of Eden or Earthly Paradise, and in that way accomplish finally God's eternal and unchanging ideal. This hope is expressed in religious terms as the "Kingdom of Heaven" or the "New Heaven and New Earth" mentioned in the Bible.

THE TWO TREES IN THE GARDEN OF EDEN: The Tree of Life and the Tree of the Knowledge of Good and Evil mentioned in the Bible are not literal trees with leaves and branches that we can find in botanical gardens. These two trees located in the center of the Garden of Eden symbolized Adam and Eve who were at the center of the divine creation. In the Bible we can find several passages

that compared man with a tree. (Prov. 11:30 and 15:4, Psalms 1:3, Is. 5:7, Dan. 4:17-19, Jn. 15:5, Rom. 11:17)
The Tree of Life was Adam's earnest desire but he could not reach it, having been expelled from the Garden after he sinned. It represents the perfected Adam or a man of life. That is why the expression "Tree of Life" is mentioned in the Bible on various occasions as the hope and permanent desire, not only of Adam, but of all human beings searching for perfection. For example, in the Old Testament - Proverbs 13:12, "... fulfilled desire is a tree of life" - and then in the New Testament - Revelations 22:14, "Blessed are those who wash their robes, that they may have the right to the tree of life..."

The Tree of the Knowledge of Good and Evil symbolized Eve in her stage of growth and her "fruit", as we will see later on, could give the knowledge of good as well as evil.

THE COMMANDMENT: The fact that the possibility of acting in a wrong direction existed indicates to us that Adam and Eve were still immature in a period of growing towards perfection. The commandment represents "God's Word, Truth or Principle" that had to guide them during their period of growth. It was the humans' responsibility to trust this word as the challenge that would enable them, by their own efforts, to reach perfection and fulfil the purpose of their lives. That story and the tragic reality in which we live today indicate to us that they failed in their responsibility.

THE FORBIDDEN FRUIT: What exactly did they do? The answer lies with the fruit. What is the meaning of this fruit that forced them towards evil? Obviously it should be the symbol of something extremely desirable for which they were willing to risk their life.

That fruit could not possibly be just a test that God put to them in order to demonstrate their obedience, as certain people believe. No parents and much less a God of love, besides being omniscient, would test their children and impose a death penalty for failing the test. Therefore, God's commandment was not a test, but a warning in order to protect his children from some serious danger.

Furthermore, our ancestors could only risk to die for something that was more tempting and stimulating than life itself. What could that be? What is more important than life itself that pushes us, even today, to risk our life? As we have already explained, only the force of love could be more powerful than the desire for life. Men and women now and in the past have sacrificed their lives for the love of God, their country, their ideals, etc. A great number of duels and deaths occurred in disputes involving a woman's or a man's love.

The fruit of a tree is a sign of its maturity and capacity for reproduction. A tree multiplies through its fruit that contains the seeds. In the same way, human beings multiply through their sexual organs which carry their seeds. Therefore, our "fruit" symbolizes the sexual love through which we also multiply ourselves. This is why, before eating the fruit, Adam and Eve did not feel ashamed of their naked bodies. Only after eating did they feel shame and hid their sexual parts. That Adam and Eve "ate of the fruit" means that they had sexual intercourse.

The fact that they hid and felt shame indicates to us that they lost their innocence and that this specific sexual relationship was carried out in disobedience to God's commandment and directions, before they achieved their physical and spiritual maturity. We have a natural inclination to hide our wickedness and feel ashamed of our wrong conduct.

Does this mean that sex itself is wrong? Of course not. On the contrary, as already explained, once we have achieved physical and spiritual maturity, sexual love centered on God should be the most beautiful and sacred experience between a man and a woman. The sexual organs should be the connecting point for the union and consummation of the true and eternal love between God, Adam and Eve. Those organs are the most valuable: The palace of love, life and lineage, through which the children of God would multiply.

God's commandment "do not eat" was necessary for Adam and Eve only during the period of their growth to perfection. Their strict obedience was very important because the realization of the Ideal of Love and the purpose of the Divine Creation depended on it. Once they reached maturity God Himself would have united with them in their enjoyment of marriage and sexual love.

THE SERPENT: We frequently encounter in most worldwide literature the famous plot of the love triangle, where two characters fight for the love of a third. Also, we find it in several of the stories about the fall. In the Bible's story this third personage is characterized as the "serpent".

Who is this "serpent" that persuaded Adam and Eve, who were pure and innocent, to have premature sexual intercourse in disobedience to God's commandment? It is obvious that this "serpent" does not refer to a literal snake with speaking abilities.

The Bible, in the book of Revelation (12:9), calls this ancient serpent the Devil or Satan and identifies it with a fallen angel who deceived the whole world and was expelled from heaven together with other angels. In the Christian tradition this leader of angels, originally good, who later betrayed God and provoked the fall of Adam and Eve, is known as the archangel Lucifer.

What did Lucifer do in order to betray the divine plan? The Bible reveals to us in verses 6 and 7 of the letter of St. Jude in the New Testament, that those fallen angels lost their position because they committed sexual sins. This indicates to us that the archangel Lucifer, as the leader of those angels, also fell and degraded himself because of a sexual sin.

Taking into consideration that this was also the sin committed by Adam and Eve upon being influenced by the archangel brings us to the conclusion that it does not refer to two separate incidents without connection, but rather they refer to the same crime.

THE FIRST CRIME OR ORIGINAL SIN

Once all the symbols of this story on the fall are examined and deciphered, we can come to the conclusion that the first crime or original sin was the adulterous and illicit relationship of sexual love between Eve and the archangel Lucifer. Afterwards, this tainted love was passed on to Adam, who was persuaded by Eve to have a premature sexual relationship with her. She corrupted him with the same type of false and selfish love learned from the archangel.

This illicit sexual love constitutes the biggest betrayal against God and His ideal of true and eternal love, which Adam and Eve were supposed to have accomplished after their physical and spiritual maturity. If love is the most sacred and valuable expectation in life, then the destruction of love represents the biggest tragedy in history.

As we will see next, this incident desecrated our first ancestors who were supposed to have set the true standard of what would be the eternal love between husband and wife. They were also meant to become the True Parents of mankind and the visible representatives of God for all their descendants, establishing a prosperous and joyful world.

But, instead, human history began with adultery and fornication, establishing a false model and a totally different example from what was meant to be the ideal, bringing human beings to a very low level, a primitive life style both physically and spiritually, reducing us for thousands of years to a caveman existence and bringing tragic consequences to human history.

We have always been taught that the original sin is the root or the source of all subsequent transgressions and is responsible for the spiritual death and misery of all humanity. Many theologians and believers have been intrigued and wondered how a single incident, whatever its gravity, could corrupt the entire human race for so long.

We could compare it to just the jab of an eye, causing permanent blindness, or to the mere perforation of the heart that finishes the life of the entire body. Psychoanalysts have often traced cases of severe mental disturbance back to a single psychic trauma or shock.

We could compare it to the contamination of the water supply, which inevitably would affect a whole city or to a disease that enters the root of a tree and gradually infects each branch and leaf. In the family tree of the human race, Adam and Eve were the root.

SIMILAR INTERPRETATIONS

The interpretation of the fall of the angels and the fall of Adam and Eve in sexual terms is not completely new in the history of Judeo-Christianity.

We find this line of interpretation in the writings of some Jewish rabbis, mostly in the inter testamental period, as well as in those of some early Church fathers and ecclesiastical writers of the first centuries.

Clement of Alexandria in the second century wrote: "... the first man of our race did not await the appropriate time, desiring the favor of marriage before the proper hour and he fell into sin by not waiting the time of God's will...they (Adam and Eve) were impelled to do it before the normal time because they were still young and were persuaded by deception." (On Marriage XIV:94, XVII:102-103).

Theophilus of Antioch and St. Irenaeus also considered Adam to be in a premature age when he violated the precept of abstaining from a sexual union with Eve, his future wife. This was not because it was a wrong action, but because it was inappropriate for their age.

This notion that the fall occurred in a period of immaturity before they achieved perfection is also shared by Peter Lombard, Hugo of St. Victor, Alexander of Hales, St. Bonaventura, John Duns Scotus and others in the Franciscan school.

Influenced by some apocryphal books of that period and especially the Book of Enoch, the notion of a carnal relationship between angels and women in the beginning of history was commonly accepted, particularly, in order to interpret verses 6:1-4 of Genesis. Tertullian (160-200) called these fallen angels "Desertores Dei, Amatores Feminarum" - Deserters of God and lovers of women.

Similar interpretations were maintained by St. Irenaeus, Athenagoras, St. Athanasius, St. Ambrose, St. Jerome, St. Justin and others. However, those ambiguous and incomplete analyses could not offer an effective solution to the serious problem of the original sin.

The "Ambrosiaster", a writing of the fourth century attributed for a long time to St. Ambrosius, but now considered to be an anonymous writing, is a little more specific on this topic:

"...Eve, the first woman, upon being corrupted, lost her virginity against the will of God and everything that was engendered by her appeared to be corrupted, starting with Cain, born of the first disobedience."

"...the devil used Eve to entangle Adam, making him an instrument in order to usurp the supreme sovereignty, which belongs only to God."

"...Adam the first and only man created and promoted by God to universal royalty, with the investiture of the divine image and likeness, accepted the devil's proposal to become like God, deflowering the virginity of his wife Eve, to whom the Lord God had promised the chaste conjugal love of a sacred marriage" (The Original Sin. Eleuterio Elorduy. B.A.C. 1977, pp. 202, 208, 221)

The "Ambrosiaster" had a great influence on St. Augustine in his interpretation of the original sin. St. Augustine, although he emphasized that the fall was primarily due to the sin of pride and disobedience, deserves our recognition for uncovering also the involvement of the sexual component, as well as his understanding that concupiscence is still the root of the present sinful state of man.

What is so remarkable about these new revelations presented now by Rev. Sun Myung Moon, is the fact that they don't appear as a mere biblical interpretation or as a study of the theological interpretations given in the past, but rather Rev. Moon proclaims with absolute conviction and great authority that these are new divine revelations, the result of a direct and intense search in the reality of the Spirit World.

Secondly, these revelations, as we will see, illuminate and deepen with precise detail, for the first time, the motivation, process, consequences and solution to this first crime or original sin which affected us so deeply and continues to affect us, tragically drawing man and woman in the direction of illicit love.

Unfortunately, we have to recognize that deep in man's heart a powerful inclination or tendency to seek an illicit or forbidden love still exists.

THE MOTIVATIONS AND THE PROCESS
OF THE HUMAN FALL

THE ANGELS

The belief in friendly spirit beings has continued in almost all cultures and religions around the world as does the fear of demonic beings.

These specific inhabitants of the spirit world are called angels in the Bible. Although religious art has often presented them as beings with wings, an angel actually has a similar appearance to us, which is why some biblical accounts confused them with human beings. The main difference with human beings is that angels never possessed nor experienced a temporal and physical body in order to grow and perfect themselves before passing to live forever in the Spirit World. But like us, angels have an eternal and indestructible spirit body, with the same faculties of emotion, intellect and will.

Angels, according to religious tradition, were created before the physical universe, assisting and serving God in the long creative process.

We find references to angels in various stories in the Bible. Sometimes they appear as messengers and emissaries sent by God and on other occasions appear to help and attend human beings to complete their mission and responsibility on the path of restoration.

Apart from these biblical references, we find a great number of testimonies about their appearance in the life of many men and women throughout history. Mohammed, St. Teresa of Avila, the Swedish scientist and visionary of the eighteenth century Emmanuel Swedenborg, just to mention a few, all had interesting encounters with angels.

Apart from the fact, already mentioned, that angels never had a physical body, another important difference with humans lies in their mission and status.

God created angels as His assistants and messengers, but He created human beings as His children. Angels were created to care for all the creation and they find their happiness in serving God and mankind, receiving our love and gratitude.

Once man and woman had achieved their perfection, they would be elevated to lords of the creation, inheriting and exercising as the visible representatives of God, a true dominion of love over everything in the physical as well as the spiritual world, including the angels.

As God's children, human beings were supposed to have authority over the angels as the Apostle Paul recognized in his letter to the Corinthians (I Cor. 6-3). But, although traditionally angels have always been perceived as glorious and superior beings, in fact human beings were originally destined to be in a superior position to any angel and only now, as a result of the fall, have the positions been reversed, which is why we perceive ourselves to be on an inferior level.

Before the creation and appearance of Adam and Eve, angels were the beings closest to God, who reflected Him to a great extent and received all His love.

THE ARCHANGEL LUCIFER AND HIS BETRAYAL

In the Judeo-Christian tradition, the Devil or Satan is the accuser and the supernatural archenemy of mankind, the origin of all evil and the initiator of all the suffering and human tragedy.

Satan is a powerful adversary, because he is a fallen angel who knows very well human weakness as well as God's plans and strategies. Since he was once Lucifer, an archangel at the heavenly court, he even has the ability to imitate God and disguise himself as an "angel of light".

He works anonymously and from behind the scenes. Satan does his most effective work as the all-pervasive, invisible, yet almost irresistible "spirit of the times". Once the devil has obscured and confused man's true situation, human values and moral standards seem to be only shadows, and what appears to be most real are concrete economic, political and material forces. Cut off from God's light, we become fearful and distrustful of others, which leads to social chaos.

Satan, therefore, benefits immensely and takes enormous advantage of man's ignorance and one of his amazing achievements is to make people believe that he does not exist.

Until the identity of a criminal is discovered, while the nature of his crime and methods remain hidden, a criminal could pretend to be innocent and it would be easy for him to continue committing crimes with impunity. But once his crime is exposed, his identity revealed and the evidence presented, everyone will be on the alert and he will not be able to continue his deception.

Next we are going to expose how this "angel of light" betrayed God and managed to take control of humanity, becoming what the Bible calls "the god of this world".

To search for the truth and fight against evil are not simple tasks. Thus it is not difficult to understand why, in this world of corruption and sin, prophets and men of God always suffered persecution and rejection.

Sun Myung Moon passed through untold spiritual battles in order to discover Satan's hidden crime and then faced enormous difficulties throughout his life in order to expose this secret to the world.

Lucifer, before his fall, was an archangel in a position of leadership in the heavenly hierarchy. Lucifer was responsible for passing God's directives and love to other angels, which is why he enjoyed a special close relationship with God, monopolizing his love.

Although chronologically, Adam and Eve appeared at the end of the creative process, Lucifer began to understand and realize very soon that they were the supreme creation of God, His more complete image. Lucifer understood that as God's children they would receive His total love once they had reached perfection and would also be the heirs and the lords of all God's creation, including the angels.

If we compare God to a king and Lucifer to the king's beloved prime minister, we can understand how the king would develop a more intimate heartistic relationship with his children than with his prime minister. His children, born as the prince and princess, would be destined to inherit all his kingdom.

Lucifer continued to receive the same love and blessings from God after the birth of Adam and Eve. However, when comparing himself with Adam, Lucifer felt disturbed and relegated from a central to a secondary position.

Lucifer particularly envied the fact that Adam and Eve, besides having a spiritual body like the angels, possessed a physical body with the capacity to procreate and have influence and dominion over the physical universe. Lucifer as servant was envious of the love they were receiving from God and jealous of the love they would consummate once they received God's blessing in marriage.

Lucifer, wishing to retain the old situation and placing more value on his former merit and position than on the love he would afterwards have received from human beings, felt as if God loved him less. Step by step he began to separate himself from God and gradually started to feel increased envy, jealousy and resentment towards this new situation.

The book *Ecclesiasticus*, which was a part of the Septuagint Bible used in the early Church and currently accepted by the Catholic Church as canonic, clearly mentioned that the Devil tempted man, motivated by envy. (*Ecclesiasticus* 2:23-24).

The *Koran* also mentions the same feeling when the angel says: "Why do I have to serve them? They are made of dust, while I am of fire " (*Koran*. Sura VII, 11)

Jealousy is a natural reaction. It is rather similar to what the first child feels when a new baby appears in the family, monopolizing all the attention of the parents. However, jealousy can be beneficial or destructive depending on our response and behavior.

Lucifer's responsibility was to remain loyal to God and have complete trust in His love and justice. He was supposed to unite with God's point of view and love and care for Adam and Eve with the same heart that God had for them, instead of seeing them as rivals.

Lucifer, who had been created first and had participated in the process of creation, had at that time much more knowledge and ability than Adam and Eve, but, in order to reach his own maturity, he had to be able to overcome his arrogance and pride.

He should have clearly foreseen that his happiness would be realized upon accomplishing his mission of serving and attending God and His children, recognizing their position, teaching them and helping them.

In this way, Lucifer acting as a good teacher for Adam and Eve, would have contributed greatly to the realization of the divine ideal.

Helping Adam and Eve to reach their perfection, would have permitted Lucifer to have an even deeper and closer understanding of God's heart, which is why this situation was necessary and beneficial to his own improvement and growth.

Once Adam and Eve had united in love with God's blessing and had become the True Parents of humanity, they would have established the model and heavenly tradition that would direct the establishment of the ideal world of eternal happiness for God, humanity, angels and all creation.

THE SPIRITUAL FALL

Unfortunately, Lucifer failed in his responsibility. It was very difficult for him to accept his new role of having to love and serve Adam and Eve with the same heart as God.

Lucifer decided to maintain his high position and importance of old and to compensate for his perceived feeling of loss of divine favor, through his desire to control Adam and Eve, and possess in the human society a position similar to that which he enjoyed in the angelic world.

Lucifer began to see this whole situation only from his own narrow point of view, moving gradually away from God and developing a selfish attitude.

Love is the source of life, happiness and beauty. The greater the love a person receives from God, the more beautiful he or she becomes. When Adam and Eve reached their adolescence, Eve became exceptionally beautiful and was able to express a special charm as the daughter of God.

Lucifer, who belonged to the opposite sex, felt a great attraction to and was stimulated by the beauty of Eve. He developed a strong desire to spend more time with her to compensate for his perceived feeling of lack of love.

Eve, for her part, saw in Lucifer the "angel of light", full of knowledge and wisdom, who could explain many things. In Eve's eyes, Lucifer seemed at that time greater and more important than her brother Adam.

Eve was fascinated by all the attention she received from Lucifer, trusting him and feeling a great admiration for him. In this way, a special attraction and love began to emerge between them.

The closer Lucifer became to Eve, proportionally the more jealousy and envy he felt towards Adam, her future husband, wanting to usurp his position.

Although Lucifer knew that his intentions were contrary to the plan of God, his desire for Eve grew stronger than his fear of betraying God. Finally, his passion and emotions became so strong that he came to the point where he was determined to challenge even God and rebel against Him.

Lucifer understood very well that love was the most powerful force, the source of life and happiness. That through love the whole ideal and purpose for the creation would be accomplished. Therefore he realized that, should he succeed in conquering Eve's love and then through her control Adam, he would finally fulfil his desire of having dominion over human society and the cosmos.

Facing this dangerous situation, God clearly warned Adam and Eve by giving them the commandment "not to eat", in order to protect them from falling into a false and illicit love relationship under the control of the archangel.

Through their obedience to the commandment they would develop and deepen their love, trust and unity with God. They would also understand the importance and the sacred value of love and accomplish, through that process, their maturity and perfection.

All this preparation would culminate in their glorious day of holy matrimony, when, with God's blessing, they would consummate their love by becoming "one single flesh" and joining themselves with God in a true and eternal love.

In this way they would establish their position as "True Parents" of humanity. They would also assure the natural subjugation of the archangel Lucifer, qualifying and becoming the lords of the whole creation, including the archangel and the entire angelic world, by their own merits.

Although Eve followed God's warnings in the beginning, resisting the archangel's advances, Lucifer was later successful in isolating her from God and Adam and he was able to influence and persuade her by creating a great confusion in her mind.

In this situation, if Eve would have asked God or consulted with Adam, she would have received the assistance and correct direction to follow, avoiding being seduced by the archangel Lucifer.

By not consulting, the power of love created by the archangel's excessive desire, plus Eve's premature desire for a complete experience of love, led Eve to the point where she consented to a sexual intercourse with Lucifer.

This illicit sex between the spiritual body of Lucifer and the spiritual body of Eve caused what the *Divine Principle* calls "the spiritual fall".

As we have already mentioned, these discoveries about the fall made by Rev. Moon, coincide with some of the interpretations given by the early Church fathers.

We also find a similar line of interpretation by several ancient Jewish commentators.

Rabbi Leo Jung, who made a careful study of the Jewish, Christian and Islamic literature on the fall, maintains that all the stories that speak of the adultery of the "serpent" with

Eve have some foundation in the Jewish tradition. (L. Jung, Fallen Angels in Jewish, Christian and Mohammedan Literature. 1974, pp 69-78)

For example, we find in the *Talmud* in Abot de Rabbi Nathan from the second century: "At that time the wicked Serpent considered in his heart and said - since I am unable to cause Adam to fall, I shall go and cause Eve to fall - He went, sat beside her and talked much with her... What did the wicked serpent plan at that moment? He thought, I shall go and slay Adam and marry his wife, and I shall be king over all the world and shall go about proudly and shall enjoy royal pleasures."

Similarly, professor F. R. Tennant of Cambridge University, who made an extensive study of the fall, comments: "It is beyond question...that various stories concerning the monstrous sexual intercourse of Adam and Eve with demons, and especially Eve with the serpent or Satan, were both widespread and ancient among the Jews. (F.R. Tennant, The Sources of the Doctrines of the Fall and Original Sin, Schocken, NY 1968, pp 156)

THE INTERRELATION BETWEEN THE PHYSICAL AND THE SPIRITUAL WORLDS

However, this explanation of the fall, in spite of how well documented it is in ancient writings and accepted in the past, presents a serious difficulty in being understood and accepted by modern man. How could it be possible for an angel to have a sexual copulation with a human being?

The Bible describes to us several incidents where angels and human spirits had direct contact with people and things. For example, Jacob received the name of "Israel" from the same angel who fought vigorously with him, dislocating his hip. (Gen. 32:25). On the Mount of Transfiguration, Jesus Christ conversed with Moses and Elijah, both of whom had died long before. (Mt. 17:3). When Mary Magdalene saw an angel next to the tomb of Jesus she considered him to be a gardener (Jn. 20:15). St. Peter could escape from prison with the help of an angel (Acts. 12:7-12).

We also find in the literature of all the great cultures and ancient civilizations similar stories in which it is assumed that people, then and there, had contact with human spirits as well as with angels.

We can conclude that angels and human spirits not only possess sensual perception as we do, but also possess a corporeal spirit form that occasionally can be perceived.

Let's consider for a moment the mystic experience of St. Teresa of Avila with an angel she called "the Heavenly Bridegroom":

"I saw in the angel's hand a long golden dart with a fiery tip. Several times he thrust it into my deepest self in such a manner that it pierced my bowels. When he drew it out it seemed as if my bowels came with him, leaving me all on fire with the great love of God. The pain was so intense that it made me moan; and yet so surpassing was the sweetness thereof that I could not wish to be rid of it".

On the other hand, we find throughout recorded history documented cases of certain individuals who had sexual relationships with spirits. We encounter unusual testimonies of people who, during the night, suffered strange sexual temptations by spirits. These are not just the well-known ejaculatory sexual dreams, commonly experienced, nor the sexual hallucinations present in schizophrenics, but real experiences while being wide awake.

In the history of religion this phenomenon is well-known and has been studied and documented. The name of "incubus", was given to a male spirit and "succubus" to a female spirit.

The anecdote from St. Anthony of Egypt is well known, that in his struggles to maintain his purity and chastity, he was tempted by spirits with the appearance of beautiful women who pursued him with all kinds of lustful, seductive and erotic tricks.

Documented cases of very similar temptations occurred often in monasteries and convents to monks and nuns who, after being shut out from the world and courageously trying to purify themselves from these desires, were confronted with and needed to pass and overcome many difficult tests.

Nor do we lack evidence of these sort of phenomena in what can be described as the satanic side.

Satanists, sorcerers and witches have long maintained that in their mystic rites one could experience sexual intercourse with their masters or supernatural confreres. During the Middle Ages, up to the seventeenth century and even until today, they confessed as much to clerical and secular authorities, not as an admission of guilt, but as part of their belief and experiences.

Of course, this type of phenomenon does not lie in the scope of the daily experience of ordinary people. It is, however a reality that has been corroborated even at the present time.

The tremendous influence of the rationalistic, pragmatic and materialistic way of thinking of modern times, turned us into skeptics and separated us from mystic experiences and intuitive awareness. It has dragged us into a deep ignorance of spiritual phenomena, not only in the field of human sciences, but surprisingly even in some religious spheres.

Since Isaac Newton, scientists thought of the universe as a great machine governed by immutable and unalterable mechanical laws. Man was said to be confined to a world of space and time which strictly limits him. Our nature and character was supposed to be rigidly determined by the interaction of heredity and environment. Our thoughts were believed to be caused by electric waves in our brains and our emotions regulated by the functioning of our glands.

Obviously such a "scientific" world view maintains almost no place for the reality of a spirit world.

However, this materialistic interpretation of science, unfortunately still believed by many, is today widely questioned. The fact of the spirit world's existence and its influence is entirely believable in the light of contemporary scientific notions and discoveries.

In the first place, our understanding of the origin and nature of the material world has been drastically altered. Although in the past scientists frequently thought that our universe had always existed without a specific beginning and reduced all that it contained to tiny solid indestructible blocks of matter, modern physicists on the contrary widely accept a beginning point of the universe and have discovered that matter consists of invisible patterns of energy.

The solidity of the material world has been proved to be totally illusory. For scientists today there is no longer a sharp distinction in drawing the line between the physical and the spiritual realms.

This mystery not only puzzled physicists but also modern neurologists and molecular biologists who had not been able to explain as yet the working of the mind-over-matter procedure in the complex processes of our brains. The eminent English neurologist and Nobel Prize winner Sir John Eccles was asked once to address a conference of parapsychologists, who were discussing the usual topics of ESP, telepathy and psychokinesis - the ability to move physical objects with the mind. If you want to see real psychokinesis, he told his audience, then consider the feats of mind-over-matter performed in the brain. It is quite astonishing that with every thought the mind manages to move atoms of hydrogen, carbon, oxygen and the other particles in the brain's cells. It would appear that nothing is further apart than an insubstantial thought and the solid grey matter of the brain. The whole trick is somehow done without any apparent link.

In the second place, depth psychology, especially that of Carl Jung, offers a different view of man. For Jung, we are not simple creatures in time and space, molded by heredity and environment. Besides being influenced by conscious thoughts and feelings, every individual is profoundly affected by a powerful subconscious realm revealed in dreams and described in ancient mythologies. This non-physical world is part of our environment and greatly affects our health and well-being. The subconscious is for Jung's psychology the spiritual world and its influences.

In the third place, scientific investigations into parapsychological phenomena have been carried out for about a century. As the careful studies of the British and American Psychic Research Societies show, a psychic or spiritual dimension does exist, verified by innumerable phenomena of extrasensory perception, clairvoyance, trance mediumship, precognition, out-of-the-body experiences in people revived from their clinical death and many other experiments that have been studied and carefully monitored, even in the former Soviet Union at the time when the official doctrine was that of atheistic materialism.

Finally, anthropologists and students of comparative cultures have begun to interpret sympathetically the religions of so-called primitive people. They have become aware of the universal belief in supernatural powers which are in contact with humans and influence their behavior.

It is ironic that all these recent discoveries, occurring in the scientific world in areas such as quantum physics, psychiatry, molecular biology, parapsychology and cultural anthropology lead us to believe again in traditional religious principles.

We do not simply continue to exist after death. From the beginning and throughout our lives, we live in both the physical and the spirit worlds. Even though most of us are not aware of this, because our spiritual senses are not open, we live surrounded by a great number of witnesses and observers. Although they are discarnate spirits, they exist all around us influencing and guiding our everyday affairs.

Roman Catholic and Eastern Orthodox theology recognize this in their doctrine of the mystical communion of saints. Catholics assert that there is a constant communion between the physical world and the spirit world. Consequently, they emphasize the importance of prayers in order to receive the intercession of the Saints, so that they continue with their concern for the spiritual health of this world.

Catholics also teach that each person has a guardian angel to help avoid evil and live righteously.

The existence and influence of numerous evil spirits are also recognized. The New Testament and the Gospels clearly show us how Jesus Christ believed in the power of demonic forces and liberated people from such influences.

MAN IS SPIRIT AND HAS A BODY

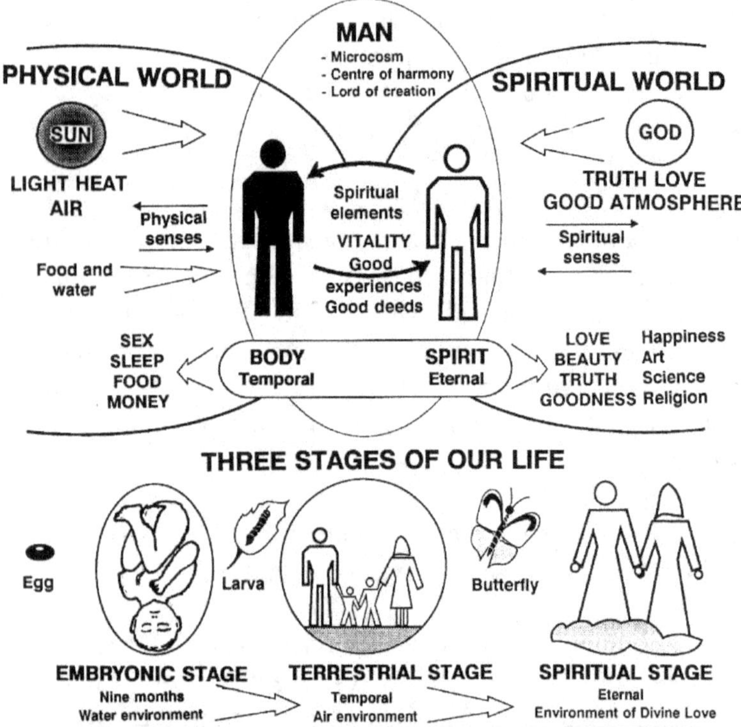

DIAGRAM 4

This kind of belief is very common to most religions in the world. In the Orient, for example, (Confucianism, Hinduism, Buddhism, Shintoism, etc.) we find ancestor worship. Ancestors are respected and asked to provide protection and good fortune.

The *Divine Principle* thoroughly agrees with this vision, and further explains that good spirits benefit from and cooperate with us, in order to accelerate our spiritual growth and the advance of world restoration in God's Providence. In exchange for this service, they themselves will advance to higher levels in the spirit world through the people whom they assist.

By contrast, evil and revengeful spirits can influence and tempt us to act in an immoral or violent manner. These spirits amuse themselves by influencing people to carry out immoral and destructive actions due to their low spiritual level and tremendous frustration and resentment.

A person under such influence should strongly resist evil impulses by confronting and overcoming them. Otherwise, no liberation from such influences can occur.

Spirits always feel attracted to people with the same level, circumstances, temperament and earthly mission as their own. Some conscious or subconscious reciprocal base must exist, however, in order for them to establish a connection.

All these observations allow us to see the close relationship that exists between the two worlds. Whether we are conscious of it or not, no one escapes this influence.

In conclusion, the above helps us to understand that the spiritual fall between Lucifer and Eve was not just an imaginary relationship or mere adultery in Eve's mind or heart, but rather the sexual act in which Eve lost her innocence and purity, affecting both of them in a very deep way.

THE PHYSICAL FALL

When love unites two beings, a reciprocal influence and change always take place in both of them.

Lucifer felt great pleasure and a selfish satisfaction after his desire of conquering and possessing Eve was fulfilled, in what can be described as the first incident of male exploitation of woman.

However, in the depth of his heart Lucifer was filled with fear and uneasiness because of having betrayed God. After rebelling against God, Lucifer lost his original position and became Satan, God's enemy.

Satan knew that this act not only violated the natural order, but totally destroyed God's purpose which was to be accomplished through Adam and Eve, the ideal of true and eternal love.

When Eve "ate of the fruit", her "eyes opened" as the "serpent" had promised. Eve received the knowledge and experience of sexual love, something unknown until that point. Through that experience, she could understand that Adam instead of Lucifer was supposed to be her true husband. She became aware of the seriousness of her actions and received the archangel's same sense of fear and uneasiness. She had separated from God, disobeying His warning.

Eve thus lost her inner peace, her dignity and sense of value as God's daughter. Anxiety, guilt, remorse, frustration, shame and other new and unknown feelings invaded her after she lost her innocence and purity.

Eve, naturally, wanted to liberate herself from the pain in her conscience and recover her old position and well-being. She thought that the best way to accomplish this was to unite sexually with Adam as his wife.

Adam, who was pure and in a state of innocence, close to God, appeared very beautiful in the eyes of Eve and at that moment represented her only hope. But instead of honestly confessing to Adam her sexual misconduct with the archangel, thus receiving comfort and requesting intercession on her behalf before God, Eve chose to hide her problem and to seduce Adam, persuading and influencing him in the same way that Lucifer had done to her.

If Eve had admitted her sin, all would have been easier. Adam would never have consented to such a premature union, contrary to God's commandment.

Once Adam had reached his maturity and perfection, he could have restored Eve by following God's guidance. As God's son, the full responsibility of avoiding the tragedy fell on Adam's shoulders. However, instead of asking God for guidance, Adam let himself be deceived and seduced.

Adam was tainted by uniting with Eve in a premature sexual relationship modeled on the selfish love learned by Eve through her adulterous relationship with Lucifer.

He was subsequently disconnected from God and also received the same elements of fear, shame and guilt.

In this way Adam and Eve both participated in what the *Divine Principle* calls "the physical fall".

This action disconnected them from God in the same way that an emotionally disturbed child is separated from reality. In this internal world of fear and shame, Satan could control and dominate our first ancestors and later their descendants.

This seduction by Eve represented the first incident of female exploitation of man and the starting point of the unnatural dominion of the body over the mind.

When virginity and innocence are lost they become irrecoverable. It is like unripe fruit that, once pulled out of a tree, cannot be put back again to continue its growing.

The premature sexual relationship of our first ancestors limited love to an immature and selfish stage, destroying the ideal of true and eternal love.

Human perfection became almost impossible to imagine as the following generations learned to live in accord with a degraded standard of love.

THE ORIGINAL SIN WAS THE CONSUMMATION OF FORBIDDEN LOVE

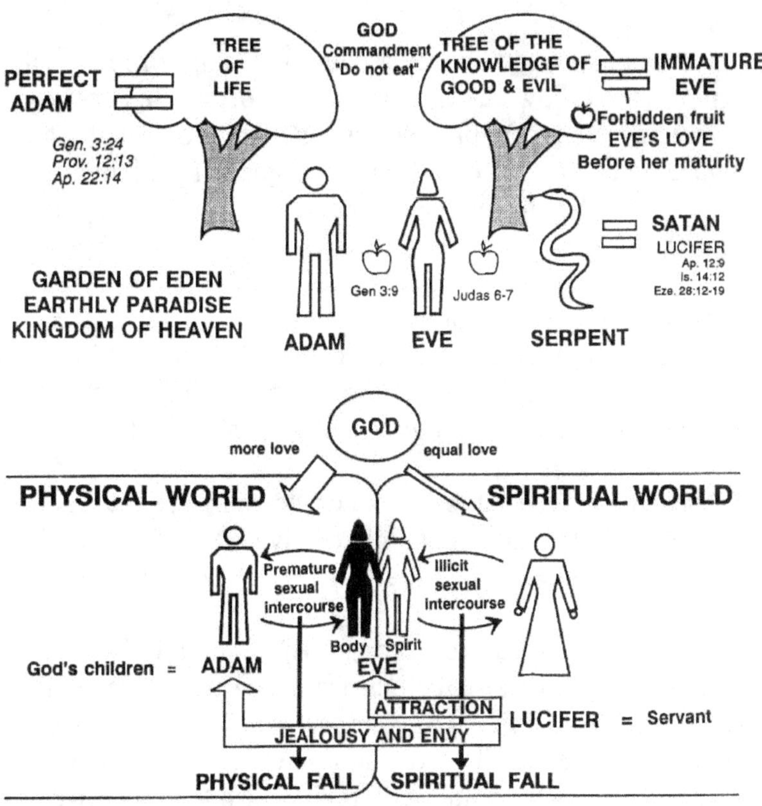

"The fall of man did not occur simply by eating a type of fruit. God asked them [Adam and Eve] to maintain their love pure until they reached perfection. The children of God united in an illicit relationship of love with God's servant, tainting themselves with a selfish love which multiplied since then from generation to generation." (SUN MYUNG MOON)

DIAGRAM 5

IMMATURE AND ILLICIT LOVE BECAME THE ORIGIN OF ALL HUMAN TRAGEDY AND SUFFERING.

The first couple established a pattern of family life for all history to follow. Adam and Eve began history by embracing each other prematurely under the control of false love taught by the fallen archangel, instead of God. In other words, they began their matrimonial life in adultery and fornication.

From that moment the problems began. Adam accused Eve of tempting him and Eve accused Adam of letting himself be seduced. Their life became one of mutual accusations, with fighting, discord, remorse and anguish.

These parents felt shame in front of the younger generation, unable to show a good example or give true orientation to the children concerning sex and love.

All this suffering had to become visible in daily life. The children inherited those feelings from the parents. They saw and listened to the fights of their parents. The children were naturally influenced by growing up in such circumstances. As a result of such an atmosphere they also fought between themselves, to the point where one brother killed the other.

The first family planted the seed of infidelity, adultery and murder. Unfortunately, human history began to develop from this model and multiplied into a world full of distrust, adultery, fornication, conflicts and murders. People learned to hurt and accuse each other rather than to love and forgive. This false tradition was passed on from generation to generation.

Because we are different from animals, human beings have few instincts to guide them. How to love and live, we learn basically in our family and culture. For this reason the pattern of behavior of the first family was essential in order to establish the true tradition that eventually would shape human life for hundreds of future generations.

Yet at the present time we continue to follow a tradition of immature, temporal, changing and conditional love which is quite contrary to what was planned originally.

Unfortunately, this incomplete and immature love is still the biggest force in the relationship between man and woman. The experience of love on this level blocks and impedes the realization of the ideal of an eternal, unconditional and unchangeable love.

At first, this love feels and promises to be authentic, but in the end we discover that it is only an imitation, in the course of time becoming incomplete and immature.

Now, as in the past, we are influenced by romantic histories, songs, poems, movies and soap operas plagued with examples of this type of false and immature love. In the famous legend of the womanizer *"Don Juan,"* we find the classical Lucifer type personage, the prototype of the conqueror and cheater of women, the "heartbreaker." This glamorous and arrogant man attracts women, seduces them, abandons them, forgets them and quickly substitutes them in a frenzied and untired experience in which he rejoices and enjoys the seduction and the conquest, but is incapable of feeling love. Literature offers us many examples of this satanic attitude of enjoying the destruction of pure, true and eternal love. In *"The Burlador of Sevilla"* of Tirso of Molina, Don Juan admits: "... the greatest of all pleasures that I could have is to deceive a woman and leave her without honor. " This attitude or tendency is completely destructive and radically opposed to true and authentic love and must be expose as such and completely eradicated.

As it occurred to Eve, it is also interesting to observe the gradual confusion, weakness and impotence of the victim of seduction. This is the response of the seduced Inés to the words of Don Juan Tenorio in it famous book of Zorrilla: "perhaps you possess, Don Juan, a mysterious amulet, that attracts me secretly like an irresistible magnet. Perhaps Satan put in you his fascinating looks, his seductive word and the love that he refused to God. And what I am going to do, but fall in your arms, oh my God! as the heart in pieces you are robbing me from here?"

Often, our relationship begins with a feeling of happiness and hope, but frequently finishes with deception, hate and resentment. Instead of liberating us and developing our spiritual potential, it makes us inhibited and distrustful.

We live in anxiety, fearing that our relationships could change, finish, or that we no longer will be able to satisfy its conditions or demands.

At the center of these situations we often find a selfish attitude. Immature love always seeks to sacrifice others for its own benefit and cannot satisfy the need in our hearts for true and unchangeable love, which we so desperately seek.

Even so, this immature love continues to be the strongest temptation for us until we reach perfection and finally experience eternal love centered on God.

The fall caused the total destruction of God's dream of true love. It degraded and changed love, the most sublime, beautiful and sacred experience, into something casual, obscene, impure and very often vulgar. Each experience of love should have been a rejoicing and heavenly explosion of energy and creativity.

The ultimate fulfillment and true satisfaction of any man or woman will be found, without doubt, in true love; nothing better can exist. Sexual intercourse between a true husband and wife is the state of true love. This union is meant to be the most valuable and beautiful, the holiest of all holy things. The experience of true love will always be the supreme experience, the climax, ecstasy of life. The anchor that will give us permanent stability. Although we can have many different experiences in the course of our life, we will always remain connected to that central anchor. Once our life on earth is ended, we will bring this lifetime anchor with us to the spirit world, where it will be anchored in the heart of God.

God made man and woman into very special privileged beings, capable of carrying out the act of love over and over again throughout their life and continuing it forever afterwards in the spirit world.

The experiences of true love are our true treasures which shape our personality, identity and character. That is the only wealth or possession we can carry with us to the spirit world.

Adam and Eve were created to be the temples where God would dwell. The human heart is the place where God should reside and manifest His love. Man's spirit body should vibrate in oneness with the love of God, directing the actions of our physical body.

True love is the power of vibration that God created in order to reach every man and woman, a force which will lead us to harmony with Him.

Therefore, Adam and Eve represented the visible and walking manifestation of the invisible God on earth. They would have been the personification of God. God wanted to live in them and through them have dominion over the whole creation. God, being invisible, cannot do all that He would desire to do. He needs us. Through each one of us He can experience love, joy and giving to others. Only working through us can He make this world into a better place. The shocking reality is that without us He is unable to establish His ideal.

This is the secret of the universe, which nobody throughout history managed to explain with the depth and clarity of the revelation received by Rev. Sun Myung Moon.

If the fall had never occurred, God would have loved Adam and Eve completely, they would have become the sacred temple where God's love would dwell forever. But Satan invaded this most sacred place. This was the worst disaster in history. That is why, the misuse of love was, still is and always will be the cardinal sin from God's point of view.

Before many religious leaders who participated in the Assembly of World Religions in August 1990, Rev. Moon asked: *"Where do God's love and man's love meet?"* In front of the silent participants, he continued: ***"In the sexual organs. That place is the palace of love, the palace of the origin of life and the palace of lineage. The power of Satan misused that place and the mission of Rev. Moon is to eliminate Satan from that place. That is the mission of Rev. Moon and the mission of religion."***

According to the original plan of God, the sexual organs would be the place where man and woman would unite and consume their eternal love centered on God.

That is the way how God planned to pass on His love, multiply life and transmit His lineage. For this reason the sexual act was supposed to be the ultimate experience where love would be sealed and consummated God, Adam and Eve would dwell together for eternity. This is the way men and women originally would have united with God.

Through that act they would create and multiply the children of God. Children are born when husband and wife unite in love, taking the form of God. Man is an instrument in order to give birth to a child; however, the power to create the children comes from God. Consequently, when husband and wife unite in the realm of God's love, they conceive, procreate and give birth to a child of God.

In the same way that each one of us could not change the parents who gave us birth, once a man and a woman get married under the absolute blessing of God, they could not be separated. They would be husband and wife on this earth and also in the spirit world, for eternity.

The starting point of the ideal world is always a perfect man and a perfect woman and their divine marriage, established with the blessing of God.

From where did humanity originate? Not from the eyes, the nose, or the head, but from the most sacred place: the reproductive organs, the organs of love, the sexual organs.

God's ideal, our existence, life and happiness, everything would be connected to that central place where love would be consummated. It is the place where true love would reside, the seed of life and true blood lineage.

We need to realize that in those organs we can locate the most valuable foundation for life, love and blood lineage. They connect the past, the present and the future.

Satan profaned that sacred place, planting his seed of corruption in the first human ancestors. That seed has been transmitted ever since, from generation to generation.

The act of sexual love between a man and a woman was always supposed to be the most sacred, pure, sublime and beautiful experience in our lives. Because this act fell under Satan's control it often turned into an obscene or vulgar experience.

Fornication, adultery, prostitution, incest, abortion, rape, pornography, homosexuality and all sexual perversions are carried out through these love organs, tainted human life in all races, cultures, religions, etc., throughout human history.

The sexual organs became the temple of evil and completely destroyed the heavenly principle. Through these organs false love, false life and false lineage were planted.

Dirty jokes and the most obscene and vulgar language are often used to describe the act of love and the reproductive organs.

The adolescent years are often spent experiencing satanic and immature love, instead of using that time in a pure and serious preparation for eternal, heavenly love.

Original love was supposed to have been the ticket to heaven for men and women, but instead a ticket to hell resulted through illicit love.

Just as a small bird knows how to build a nest, we were supposed to know how to build true love relationships. Due to the fall, human beings should be embarrassed before some of the lower forms of the creation. After choosing their mate, certain animals remain faithful and, in some cases, even after one partner's death, remain celibate.

How is it possible, that the loyalty and fidelity of rational and spiritually conscious man is so much weaker than the instinct of an animal?

Animals do not commit sins. They live within the natural law which governs the universe. On the other hand, the supreme creation of God became morally degraded to a level far lower than animals. Massacres, torture and sadism are inflicted on each other by human beings throughout recorded history. This has no parallel with any conduct known in the animal kingdom, not even amongst the most terrible predators. Nor do animals rape or engage in prostitution, homosexuality and a whole range of sexual perversions.

We read in the Bible that God, seeing the wickedness and perversity of man, was sorry that He created man and felt sadness in His heart (Genesis 6:5-6).

THE HEART OF GOD

The worst part about this tragedy is the impact it had on God Himself. Let's read some comments in this regard given by Rev. Sun Myung Moon in several sermons:

"The biggest irony is that Adam and Eve did not deeply understand how much pain and suffering their actions were actually causing God, and since then no one has ever understood God's anguished heart at the moment of Adam and Eve's fall. The fall was the pinnacle of the suffering of God ". (22 May 1977)

"God wished that the entire universe had broken into pieces rather than Adam and Eve. If His entire creation had been destroyed then God would not have been as sorrowful as over Adam and Eve. If the whole earth had broken into pieces God could easily have recreated a home for Adam and Eve, but God cannot recreate love; it has to be restored and be given voluntarily and with free will. The entire purpose of creation focuses upon one man and one woman, and if they broke into pieces then there is no hope, only total darkness. God cannot create them again. He has only one course to follow: restoration." (31 Dec. 1978)

"God's position is almost like that of a husband whose wife betrays him and runs away with some stranger. After loving her so much, what feeling would that man harbor in his heart towards her? He would feel tortured." (1 April 1979)

"In a certain sense, Eve was supposed to be the future wife of God. This is so, because once Adam would have reached the level to be one with God, the Spirit of God would have dwelled within him, then Adam would be the embodiment of God Himself. Consequently, for God His wife was raped by Satan." (4 Feb. 1969)

"Satan is the archangel, nothing more than a servant of men and God, but this servant not only raped the daughter of God; he took away all the master's property as well. Satan is an impostor and a fornicator -an adulterer. Our job is to expose and expel Satan from our planet. However, so far in

human history, Satan has been trying to kick God out of the planet." (27 Aug. 1987)

"The deepest sorrow in God's heart in all of history was Adam becoming a fallen man. And secondly, the death of Jesus Christ." (11 Feb. 1972)

"Have you ever stopped to think how you would feel if your spouse and children were kidnapped? This is exactly how God feels in His heart. In God's eyes all men have been taken away and He is desperately anxious to bring them back." (11 June 1978)

"The fall of man was in the very place where God was supposed to dwell. But he was expelled. Satan became the owner. He became the occupant. Therefore, the crime of Satan is the destruction of love which is the true essence of God. Consequently, God could not forgive Satan, because if He does, it would mean that Satan himself is destroying God. It is as if Satan is in the position of the invader of a residence. He came to the temple of God, snatched His position, enslaved man and threw out God." (London 1972)

Young Whi Kim, one of the first followers of Rev. Sun Myung Moon writes:

"Through the fall of man, God lost His beloved children who were created in His image as His substantial bodies. When God saw this tragedy, He could not bear it. His heart was broken and He felt the greatest sorrow. God created man to be such a loving being, and God poured out everything He had, His heart, love and energy to make men His children, the masterpieces of all His creation.

Man was created as such a valuable being that without man, God's ideal could not be realized. However, God lost His children through the fall.

God also lost the whole creation, because human beings, as the lords of creation, were dominated by Satan. God's purpose and ideal of creating man and the universe was to receive joy and happiness by having a relationship with them.

God lost everything, and because of this God came to have no one who could completely reflect His nature. Instead God saw the most hateful relationships develop between fallen people and Satan. Men and women who were created to be God's children became Satan's children. Human beings, who were created to be the lords of all creation, became the servants of servants.

However, fallen men do not know their miserable state and often remain satisfied. As ignorant orphans, they even deny the existence of God and do all kinds of evil, establishing a tragic world. So, God lost not only His children, but rather God's children came to stand against Him as His enemies.

God stands in a paradoxical position: He cannot refuse fallen men because they were created as His children originally by Him, and He cannot fully love them, because they became evil children. He cannot destroy them, but must work to save them from the fallen state to the original state of creation.

When God sent His prophets or representatives and even His beloved Son, humanity just opposed them, stoning and killing them and the opposite happened, increasing God's sorrow and pain.

God's expectation for man was so great when he began His work of creation that the disappointment, sorrow and anguish which God felt when man fell were indescribable. We cannot find anyone more grievous than God. Whenever God sees the reality of this world, it constantly reminds Him of the fall of man and makes Him sorrowful. God desperately wants to have His children restored and wants to love them.

That is why He is doing the restoration or salvation work throughout history. Consequently, we should console Him and end His suffering, restoring our original position as His children."

The favorite word that Jesus Christ used in order to call God was "Abba" which means "father". Not only is God a close father to us, but He is also impatiently waiting for our return, as Jesus Christ taught us in the prodigal son's parable.

Through the thousands of years of human history God has never received true glory and happiness from men. Through the silence of centuries God lived in agony with a broken heart.

How long and deep have been His consternation, distress and sorrow!

In the Bible the prophet Hosea describes to us the following feelings of God:

"But the more I called Israel, the further they went from me. They sacrificed to the Baals and they burned incense to idols. It was I who taught Ephraim to walk, taking them by the arms, but they did not realize it was I who healed them. I led them with cords of human kindness, with ties of love;

I lifted the yoke from their neck and bent down to feed them. (Hosea 11:2-4).

God reveals to us through the prophet Isaiah: "The ox knows its owner, and the ass its master's crib; but Israel does not know, my people do not understand" (Isaiah 1:3).

Separated from God, humanity from its side, has been suffering of hunger and thirst in spirit, as Psalm 42: 2-4 reads:

"As the deer pants for the streams of water, so my soul pants for you. Oh God! My soul thirsts for God, for the living God: When can I go and meet my God? My tears have been my food day and night."

The separation from God brought man's spiritual death, causing misery, tragedy and evil to all humanity.

Since then, many religions have developed in human society. We look for God through Jesus Christ and other sacred persons. In one way or another, any religious search represents the human effort to restore the image of God within ourselves. This search demonstrates that man's deepest desire is to find God and establish a relationship with Him.

Had man not fallen, humanity would have experienced the love of God, walking and creating with Him. All religious practice would be unnecessary, just as a healthy man does not need a doctor or medicine.

Except for the passages mentioned in Isaiah, Hosea, the Psalms and Jesus Christ's parables, which hardly showed God's grievous heart, our Heavenly Father's deep pain has always remained hidden.

Just as it is very difficult for us to reveal our innermost feelings to everyone, because most people would fail to understand what we were talking about, God could not reveal completely His deep sorrow and anguish, except to someone who would understand exactly what Satan had done and its effect on God's whole plan.

In his deep spiritual exploration, Sun Myung Moon discovered the details about what happened originally, uncovering for the first time the root of this age-old hidden grief of our Heavenly Father, His innermost feelings, His unresolved pain and anguish, and His indignation which He could not express for such a long time.

Once Sun Myung Moon was aware of Heavenly Father's situation and shared His untold and hidden heart, he cried endlessly over God's anguish for days on end. After that he could no longer remain silent or indifferent.

This type of heart was his constant motivating power, which moved him to persevere with determination and courage in spite of the enormous difficulties he had to confront. With a feeling of terrible urgency, he has been constantly working throughout his life, inspiring others to unite in this cosmic battle to overcome and completely eliminate evil and sin from man's life.

For Unificationists, the purpose of salvation is not merely to obtain the divine forgiveness of our individual personal sins and go to heaven. Unfortunately, so many people still believe this and fail to recognize that true salvation means the restoration of the entire human race. It means returning each and everyone of God's children, liberating them from vice, sin and suffering. Only in this way will the final goal, our Heavenly Father's liberation, be accomplished.

From his youth, Sun Myung Moon was absolutely determined to unravel and heal the intolerable burden in the heart of God and uncover the causes of God's deep grief. The task to end and solve this cosmic tragedy became his lifelong mission.

Once God is free to exercise His loving sovereignty over creation, His great and endless joy will bring about a cosmic springtime. The entire universe will be forever radiant in happiness and harmony.

THE ABSOLUTE AND SACRED POWER OF LOVE

We need to remember that the concept of love was first and central in God's mind. His ideal for humanity was not to plan a world of laws and regulations, but a world of love. Therefore, love was established by God as the absolute power, superior to any other power.

Love is the supreme power in the universe. God made this power so absolute that even His principle, that regulates the working of the universe, does not exclude the possibility of expressing love in a form that violates His will.

Literature and history alike pay tribute to this omnipotent reign of love over the human heart. Shakespeare immortalized how the force of love drove Romeo and Juliet to suicide, how Hamlet's uncle was driven and blinded by passion to kill his brother in order to marry his sister-in-law and how Lear became literally insane because he made a mistake about how much his daughters loved him.

In our time, we have seen how King Edward VII of England abdicated the throne for the sake of love.

Religious psychologists point out that in this fallen world the erotic impulse itself is strong enough to disregard all the moral conventional norms which society and conscience ascribe to the will of God.

The power of love was the only conceivable force that could cause man to deviate from his path to perfection. When Eve succumbed to the seduction of the rebellious archangel and prematurely united with Adam, both of them were still under the indirect dominion of the love of God.

They abandoned God and His ideal in order to follow their personal desires. They did not put themselves in a position to trust, wait and sacrifice as was required in order to attain true love which becomes perfect.

God could not exercise direct dominion over them before they reached perfection. Once Adam and Eve had attained maturity, no one and nothing could have broken their unconditional love towards their Creator.

Only at that stage could God freely pour His infinite love upon them. Until that time, the love of our first parents for God was incomplete and could be misdirected.

For this reason, a man and a woman should experience full union of love with each other, only once their individual love for God has become unconditional.

Without succeeding in perfecting our love for God, true affection for another human being is difficult, as the marital problems of our time clearly demonstrate.

WHY GOD DID NOT INTERVENE

If God is all-powerful, all-knowing and all-good, why did He not somehow protect Adam and Eve from frustrating His plan for the creation?

The *Divine Principle* suggests that this problem must take four factors into consideration: Human freedom, the absolute and sacred power of love, the spiritual immaturity of Adam and Eve and humanity's intrinsic dignity as the lord of creation.

We possess freedom because we are created in the image of God. If we are human, we are responsible for our actions. If we lack free will we become mere puppets controlled by others.

God's omnipotence is not absolute and His power is limited by the freedom that He gave to man. According to this point of view, man and God must work together to realize the goal of history.

True love by definition is free and voluntary. We cannot force anyone to love us. Not even God could violate this principle.

God wanted Adam and Eve to choose freely the way of goodness and decide to love God in response to His love for them.

True love can be born only if freedom exists. If God had intervened in the fall, He would have invalidated the meaning and value of His children. He would have violated His own perfect system and would have nullified human responsibility. Our freedom, responsibility and creativity have an absolute value which God recognizes and respects unconditionally.

Human beings were created as the lords of creation and potentially possess a greater dignity than any other creature. So in order to be completely qualified for that position, they have to rely on their own powers and judgement in perfecting their hearts according to the divine image.

OUR VALUE AND DIGNITY

- WE ARE MADE IN GOD'S IMAGE

- WE ARE THE VISIBLE MANIFESTATION
  OF THE INVISIBLE CREATOR

- WE HAVE THE VALUE AND DIGNITY
  OF GOD'S SONS AND DAUGHTERS

- WE ARE ETERNAL BEINGS

- WE HAVE A UNIQUE VALUE
  No two persons are exactly alike.
  Each of us is a unique masterpiece.

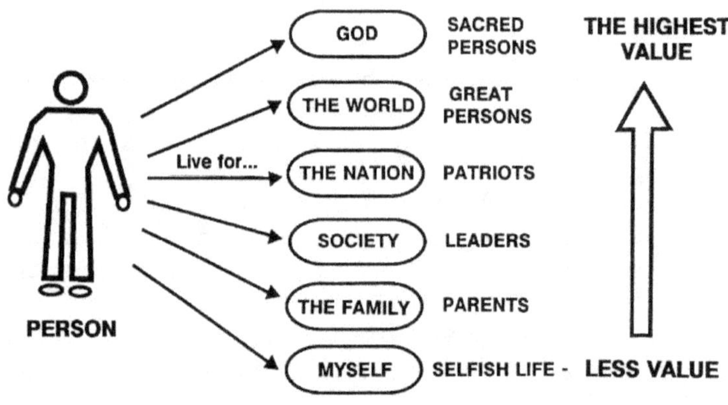

God, being invisible, cannot do all that He would desire to do. He needs us.
Through each one of us He can experience love, joy and give of Himself to
others. Working through us He can make the world a better place. The shocking
reality is that without us God is unable to establish His ideal.

DIAGRAM 6

God waits until man learns how to govern himself, before permitting him to govern the world. We must have dominion over ourselves first before we can have dominion over creation. To stand with dignity before God and creation, we must act of our own volition. In this way, God wants man to share in His creative work.

Man must pass through a process of maturity, during which time great responsibility is received in order to develop self-initiative and self-discipline. We have to grow to a secure state worthy of the trust of God, our fellow men and all the creation, including the angels.

From this perspective of human responsibility we can understand that the human fall was man's affair alone. God is in no sense a responsible participant. He cannot recognize false love and evil as part of His own creation. In the same way as certain actions which violate the constitution and laws of a country cannot be accepted as valid. In the same way that nations refuse to recognize illegitimately established governments, God could not recognize the world resulting from the fall.

To intervene to stop an action outside His perfect principle would be equivalent to recognizing it as something valid as a part of his creation. If God had acted, it would have implied recognizing Adam and Eve as mature beings when they were not. God can only have direct dominion over mature sons and daughters who have achieved spiritual maturity through fulfilling their portion of responsibility. To interfere prior to their perfection would deny Adam and Eve's ability to achieve perfection on their own.

For all these reasons, irrespective of how painful and unbearable His heart must have felt at that moment, God could not intervene and prevent the fall.

THE HISTORICAL CONSEQUENCES OF THE FALL

Due to the fall, the first human family separated from God and fell under the influence of the rebellious archangel. With the misdirection of love, a false tradition and false way of life appeared. From that moment, evil habits and sin multiplied through the first family's descendants.

As a result a "world" outside God's principle, opposed to His ideals and outside His control, developed. Using a religious term, we refer to the world of vice, confusion, poverty, exploitation, war and suffering as "Hell".

Humanity, separated from God, without true laws and in a state of disorder, became brute-like and degraded. In the absence of a common purpose and ideal, men were alienated and gradually lost their identity. Human beings, upon losing their spiritual light, fell into a state of savagery with a spiritual sensibility as dull as that of animals.

Fights and conflicts isolated humans more and more. This resulted in division and continuous separation. It created and increased the territorial barriers of communication, accelerating notable differences in race, language, belief, customs, etc. which characterized human history. The fall reduced humanity to a primitive ignorant state of barbarism which stagnated human moral and material development.

However, notwithstanding the lowering of spiritual standards, humanity always kept within them the good potential of our original nature. God was, therefore, able to work through our conscience, gradually developing and elevating our heart and intellect.

God has been inspiring us to fulfil our responsibility. Since the dawn of history, God has been the hidden force that has guided the plan to restore this world of sin to its original state and recover His lost ideal.

God, our Creator, has a Will. That Will is to restore this world to one of true love and peace. Ultimately, He will restore His original ideal world, re-creating it from the present circumstances of this world.

Consequently, from this point of view, human history has a direction and a goal. That goal is the restoration or the spiritual re-creation of mankind from the fallen state to the original state. History's objective is thus to convert "Hell" into the "Kingdom of Heaven".

Traditionally so much has been said about salvation. But, what is salvation? Salvation is precisely that: restoration. A doctor saves a patient by helping him to recover or restore his lost health. This process requires the cooperation of both the doctor and the patient.

God's efforts throughout history reflect a similar situation. Although God is all-powerful, He could not save humanity by His power alone, as man's cooperation and effort are also necessary. History is therefore the record of the efforts of God and man, of both successes and failures, in response to the help of God.

Why does God want to save us in spite of the fact that we are the ones who betrayed and abandoned Him, creating this world of hell and tragedy? There are three fundamental reasons:

First, because God is all-powerful and absolute. When He decides to achieve His goal, ultimately nothing or no one will stop it. He will never be defeated by Satan. If God is all-powerful, the least that He would be capable to accomplish would be to create a world of peace and happiness for humanity. If this type of world could not be realized, then we could conclude that God does not exist.

Secondly, <u>God created human beings as His children</u>. Although we have betrayed Him many times, God is our True Father. He could not abandon us. His happiness is completely dependent upon us. Just as human parents feel the most concern and sympathy for the son or daughter who suffers most, God's concern draws Him to His children who suffer. Because of true love God could not separate Himself from our misery. The all-powerful Creator is also our loving Father who suffers with all of us. For this reason He will definitely resolve the problem of the fall.

Thirdly, <u>God created the human spirit to be indestructible and eternal</u>. Therefore, even if this physical world were destroyed, the spirits of innumerable people who lived in the past would remain in the spirit world unable to be liberated. Until humanity is restored physically and spiritually, the results of the Fall will not be solved and these people cannot be restored.

The record of God's efforts to save humanity is registered in the history of world religion. In fact, the word religion comes from the Latin word "religare" which means rebind. The true purpose of religion, therefore, is to unite man again with God and restore His original ideal.

The religious nature of man we see from the time of the earliest paintings of primitive man, who already described spiritual beings and forces. God was able to elevate humanity's intellectual and moral level stage by stage. Higher religious expressions developed, reflecting a progress in restoration. As the fall removed us from the Truth, we must recreate ourselves by the Word or Truth in the process of restoration.

That is why God always works through righteous and sacred persons, through prophets and spiritual leaders who appeared progressively throughout history to explain the divine truth. When we observe the common points and the gradual unification of ideals in the history of religion, we can see God as the inspiring source.

In his profound study on the evolution of cultural spheres, Arnold Toynbee discovered that cultures have always developed around a religion. Whenever a more universal and elevated religion developed, a higher form of culture also appeared, eventually reaching out to and absorbing the neighboring cultures of a lesser level. Those people and nations in history which could not advance to a higher religious philosophy were always absorbed.

In the past our world consisted of more than twenty six different cultural spheres, which in the course of history united to create the present world's four great fundamental cultural spheres: Hinduism-Buddhism, Judeo-Christianity, Islam and the cultures of the Far East, Confucianism-Taoism-Shintoism.

The conclusion of Arnold Toynbee is that, in fact, we are moving toward one single worldwide culture. Increasing means of communication will further accelerate this process. For the *Divine Principle* this is not a coincidence, but the result of God's and man's efforts to recreate a unified world that strives to restore God's eternal and unchanging ideal.

The scientific developments and technology that we enjoy today are extraordinary. We have the capacity and the external means to construct a marvelous world of comfort and well-being for all humanity. However, in spite of this great potential, we are not yet capable of building a harmonious world of peace and happiness because there has been no parallel development on the spiritual and moral level.

An imbalance exists between our external know-how and our internal development. For example, although we left the Earth to explore outer space and have succeeded in putting men on the moon, we are still incapable of living and successfully applying, ethical and moral norms such as the Ten Commandments given by God to Moses approximately 4,000 years ago.

In spite of all our progress, we are still not fulfilling our role as the true lords of creation, protecting the precious inheritance that God gave us. In fact, because of our fallen nature we have even mistreated nature and prevented it from fulfilling its proper function.

Instead of existing in harmony with the environment, human selfishness and greed have led us to exploit nature irrationally, generating a hostility.

The Apostle Paul talks about this suffering of nature which he compares with the pains of childbirth, anxiously waiting for the revealing of the children of God (Rom. 8:22). And not only nature, but also God and all humanity are waiting for that great change and transformation which will allow us to recover our value and dignity as God's children and realize a world free of evil and sin.

The majority of thinking people surely agree that we need a profound transformation to liberate us from chaos, immorality, violence and corruption.

But, with few exceptions, the general tendency until now, has been to look first at the problems we see outside of ourselves; we want to "see the straw in the other's eye". That is why so much hope was placed in the belief that certain programs or political and economic systems would give us the ultimate solution.

For example, when the Bolshevik revolution triumphed in 1917, it created great expectation and its leaders were proud to end an old system of exploitation and impose a new one which promised justice and peace. Today, the whole world is witness to the tragedy of that system and its subsequent failure.

The great lesson we can learn from this and similar experiences in the past is that it is illusory to pretend that we first have to change society and its structures so that later those changes will necessarily transform human conduct.

No new plan, program or system can work if it is guided by the same corrupt people. Unless man changes, nothing will change. The root of human problems begins with the selfish attitude of the individual on whom the structures and systems of society are built. Only when man is capable of overcoming selfishness in himself will it be possible to foresee permanent and stable changes in society.

THE SOLUTION OF WORLDWIDE PROBLEMS BEGINS WITH THE INDIVIDUAL

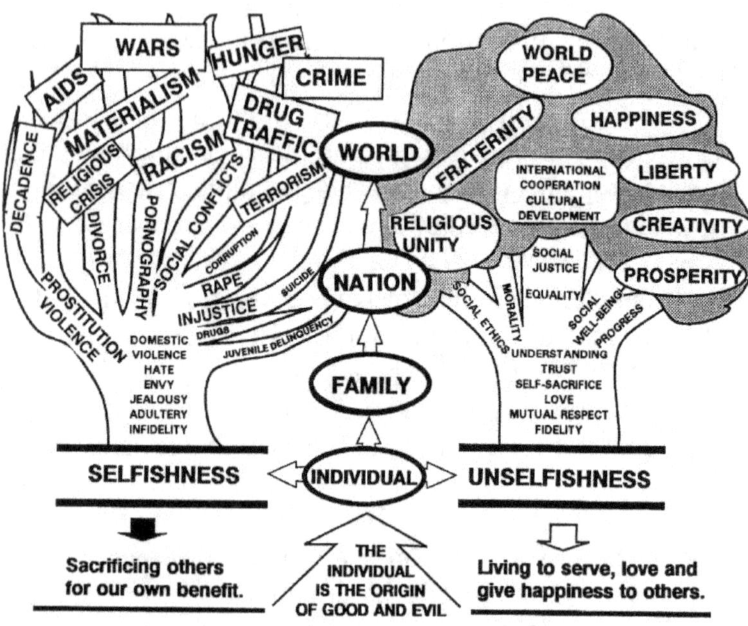

"I can foresee a great change, a revolution coming to the world, not by fire or bullets, but by the truth of God kindling men's hearts. I have come to ignite this spiritual revolution, a quiet revolution that changes man from selfishness to unselfishness." (Sun Myung Moon)

DIAGRAM 7

That is where humanity should direct its hope and dreams of true peace in the future. The will of God is to eradicate selfishness in each individual, and then to transform and re-create humanity in His own temple, so that all people become sacred.

True worldwide peace and harmony between nations therefore does not begin on the national level, but in the perfection of the individual. Each person is perfected upon being converted

into a temple of God. This is where worldwide peace starts. Each one of us is the true starting point of worldwide peace and the ideal world.

We need to completely restore our spiritual sensitivity, so that we can never mistreat or harm others. We must come to feel the suffering and pain of others as our own. In the same way, our happiness also will be achieved when we make others happy.

In the original world of God's creation, man fighting man would be like the right hand fighting the left, or even worse, like your own hand pulling out your own eyes. In the ideal world there would be no conflict, no evil. There would only be harmony, cooperation and mutual assistance. There would be unity among people in the pursuit of truth, goodness and beauty. This would truly be the world of peace that humanity is seeking.

We have to recognize, therefore, that of all the transformations which affected the destiny of history, the biggest and most important transformation has yet to be realized.

Of all the battles that have ever been fought, the most fundamental one is yet to come. That is the struggle in which each one of us individually has to finally overcome the evil within ourselves and become free. We must thus purify and liberate ourselves from sin. To be more specific, we must erase false and illicit love completely from our heart and memory. Such love has poisoned humanity for such a long time.

These profound revelations about the origin of immorality and evil are of vital importance, as they clarify to us the nature of sin. They give us the weapons and knowledge to overcome it.

The last and most difficult revolution will be the internal revolution of our heart and conscience. It will carry us from injustice, corruption and selfishness to an attitude of love and service to others as the supreme value.

As Rev. Sun Myung Moon prophesied:
"I can foresee a great change, a revolution coming to the world, not by fire or bullets, but by the truth of God kindling men's hearts. I have come to ignite this spiritual revolution, a quiet revolution that changes man from selfishness to unselfishness."

Sun Myung Moon, in his inaugural address to the Federation for World Peace in August 1991, in Seoul, Korea, in front of presidents and dignitaries of many countries, proclaimed:

"The twenty-first century shall be a righteous century. In the twenty-first century wealth will not be the dominating factor. Instead, the human soul and spirit shall be predominant. The twenty-first century shall be the era of unity between God and man. It shall be the era when a new

awakening will come to every person, a realization that we shall benefit more when we genuinely live for the sake of others. In the twenty-first century selfishness will decline. Life, honor and glory based on unselfishness shall be triumphant. These are the characteristics of the coming twenty-first century. The era for peace is approaching. And much more, the opportunity for the realization of the Kingdom of Heaven on earth will be at hand. The twenty-first century shall be a hopeful and glorious century."

The Bible speaks of "the last days" and of the "end of the world." If history had begun in goodness, it would not be necessary to end. But because history began with evil, the last days have to come about in which evil will be finally eradicated and an end will come to the world of vice and sin. It will be the time to which the Holy Scriptures refers to as that "of beating our swords into ploughshares". In other words, a time of transition when "hell" will be transformed into the "Kingdom of Heaven."

There will not be a literal destruction of the universe through catastrophes, as some Christians have maintained. The last days will be a time of happiness when mankind's greatest hope, firmly maintained throughout history, will finally be realized.

THE FIGHT BETWEEN THE MIND AND THE BODY

In order to win this final battle of history and be victorious in subduing and eradicating evil within ourselves, it is necessary to clearly recognize our weakness, selfishness and fallen nature.

Just as Satan controlled the first human ancestors through their physical desires, he continues to control us through our selfish physical desires.

The fall, which came about through false love, created a discord between unselfish direction of the mind and selfish misdirected physical desires. This resulted in disunion and struggles in our vertical relationships - with God, our parents, our juniors, our students - and also in our horizontal relationships - with our spouse, our companions, our friends, our colleagues, etc. These relationships, instead of being characterized by genuine love, became frequently distorted because of the confusion that exists within ourselves, between the desire of the mind to serve others and the physical desires to satisfy oneself.

Originally, the mind and body were supposed to be united and unable to separate. The human mind represents the mind of God. The human body is the recipient that accommodates the mind, it is the place where the mind dwells. The separation between these two occurred at the time of the Fall and caused the human body to come under the domain of Satan and selfishness.

Our physical body is important, mainly to support our spiritual growth. On its own, the body only seeks for its own comfort and well-being. That is why evil always seeks to mobilize our body in order to dominate and nullify the desires of our mind. In the beginning illicit sexual love gives us the illusion and feeling of unity and happiness as if it is true love. Money, power and fame can also give us the illusion of fulfilling our internal desires through external means. We often do wrong things only in order to satisfy our own desires and physical necessities, even at the cost of harming others.

On the other hand, in our mind, the human conscience became the agent of God. The conscience does not exist for our own benefit. It is implanted so we can act with righteousness. It always seeks goodness and follows the altruistic way. But the body often rebels against the conscience. The body only seeks its own comfort and is inclined to act selfishly, carrying out its carnal desires. The conscience, on the other hand, deals with correcting the body and subjugating it in the direction of the mind. For that reason, it is inevitable that we experience conflict and internal struggles within ourselves.

God exercises His influence in order to stimulate our mind through our spiritual desire. Our spiritual desire searches for true satisfaction through good and responsible activities. We are happy making others happy first.

Our body, however, is often attracted to alternative ways and seeks to go in another direction. When something important is to be done, the body asks for rest, food or drink and the person who is not strong or spiritually developed will say: "I want to do these things and I should do them", but the one who is truly wise will say: "This entity with its desires is not the real "I" and must wait." Often when the opportunity to help someone appears, the body says: "Why bother? It is better if someone else does it instead of me," but we should respond to our body: "You will not prevent me from doing a good deed."

The body is in our service, the horse on which we ride. Consequently, we should treat it well and look after it, we should feed it properly and keep it clean. Without a healthy and clean body we cannot carry out the arduous tasks which will allow us to reach spiritual perfection. But, we should always be the one who dominates our body and not let the body dominate us.

In a way, our worst enemy is our own body. We should firmly establish this principle: "I must dominate myself first before I have dominion over anything else." If I am controlled by my circumstances, it means that my body is controlling my mind. But if I can maintain my position and mental state, irrespective of where I go or how difficult the circumstances, it means that my mind controls my body.

The clash of mind and body within ourselves represents the war between good and evil.

The mind must have the internal strength and the necessary spiritual power of self-control to overcome the desire for food, sleep and sex, which are the three most basic desires of our body.

That is why the traditional religions of the world, unanimously, teach the principle of corporal discipline through fasting, prayer, sexual abstinence, etc. - doing things that the body does not desire to do. Religion is the training ground where the unruly desires of the body are controlled, steering the body in accordance with the will of the mind. A true religion emphasizes self-denial, self-control, discipline and teaches to live sacrificially for others. There has never been any great religion in history that emphasized selfishness or self-centeredness. Religious people who lived in convents and monasteries submitted themselves to an ascetic life of strict discipline.

We see that Buddhist monks often sit down to meditate for years and years, trying to remove from themselves all physical desires, to the point of emptiness. By doing that, they want to find the ideal standard of human character. Their entire effort could be described in a single phrase: They deny the small selfish "I" in order to find the true internal self. This is their purpose.

However, no one is capable of completely controlling the body without uniting internally with God. Only when our mind is united with the power of God's love and truth can we use our bodies correctly. The mind has to be in the subject position and the body in the object position in relation to the mind. The love of God and His truth has the power of harmoniously uniting them together. Such a person of unity is described in religious terms as a saint. That is why religion has been God's instrument to guide and restore man to His original ideal.

Originally, God made us with the capacity to live in happiness. We were created to be intoxicated not by drugs but by the love of God. Since we lost this original capacity, we have been searching for unnatural and artificial means of intoxication such as alcohol or drugs. However, man and woman were created to intoxicate each other with love centered on God. There is nothing that surpasses this feeling of joy and happiness. Each cell of our body will explode with delight. The eyes, ears, all the tissues of the face, the arms and legs will be reborn to live in a rapture of happiness.

Once people discover the way to be intoxicated with true love centered on God, even if they are pushed to use drugs, alcohol, etc., they will refuse them. It will seem worthless in comparison. Once men and women grow to perfection and are united with God's True Love, no power under the sun can break that. It would be impossible for men and women to be unfaithful to one another. The mind would be completely in control. If your discipline is such that your conscience wins over the dictates of your body, including the temptation of illicit love, then you shall win a ticket to heaven.

OUR ORIGINAL NATURE AND OUR FALLEN NATURE

The famous scientist and spiritualist of the 18th century, Emanuel Swedenborg visited and explored the spiritual world for nearly 30 years. Once he was thinking about heaven and hell and he wrote this answer given to him by teachers there:

"There are three basic facts about hell, but they are just the opposite of the facts about heaven. The basic facts of hell are three loves -- the love of ruling due to self-love, the love of having what belongs to others due to love of the world, and the love of fornication."

"The basic facts of heaven are the three loves opposite to these -- the love of ruling due to a love of being useful, the love of having worldly goods due to a love of putting them to good use, and real married love"

As we can see, heaven and hell begins with me, with our loves and attitudes. Consequently, it is everyone's responsibility to really recover and maintain the proper attitude over the **four original and God-given desires** to fulfill the purpose of our lives.

These four original desires are:

1. **The desire for sexual love.** The proper way to fulfill this desire is to keep the basic law of the cosmos, which was given already in the very beginning with the symbolic expression "do not eat". This means abstinence before marriage and to maintain absolute fidelity and love to our spouse after marriage, accomplishing the ideal of an eternal love and a family that will give us the greatest peace and happiness forever.

On the contrary, the misuse of this natural desire brings about a love for variety or free sex, in other words, love of fornication and adultery, that is opposed to a real married love. In the end, people involved in this type of love never find permanent satisfaction, and it inevitably leads them to unhappiness.

2. **The desire for material things (love of having worldly goods).** There is nothing wrong with our wish to own things, to be rich, wealthy and prosperous, to be a millionaire, to have money, land and property.

   All of these aspirations are related to the desire to exercise a true and loving dominion over the environment that will enable us to be the true lords or caretakers of the creation. But what is the proper attitude to realize these desires? If everything we possess is used correctly for the benefit and service of others, bringing joy and happiness to everyone and harmony to the environment, that is perfectly fine. On the other hand, if we hold possessions only for our own personal interests and self-gratification, that is unprincipled and in the end it will bring neither joy or lasting prosperity.

3. **The desire for authority (love of ruling).** Everyone wishes to be a king or queen. This is a natural and original desire because of our position and dignity as children of God. The proper way to exercise this desire is to become a true leader. A true leader is the one who delights in being useful and sincerely serves and loves others the most. Therefore, such a person is naturally appreciated and everyone will gladly give him or her that recognition, power and position.

   Value and Position. When we have true internal value in ourselves and the external qualifications, soon or later, position will be given to us even if we do not seek for any appointment. On the contrary, when someone cherishes a position for his or her own benefit or self-glory, and obviously lacks moral value, in the long run such person will lose that position.

4. **The desire for self-perfection.** This is an original desire or ambition that will always motivate us to reach our potential as children of God.

We all have this desire to be good and successful. We like to gain knowledge and develop skills. We want to achieve excellency in the things we do. We like to be recognized, to be admired and be famous. We wish to become great performers, artists, scientists, lecturers, sports champions, inventors, philanthropists, etc.

As mentioned above, the proper attitude to realize all these aspirations is to use all our achievements for the good and happiness of others. If not, our desire, ambition and hope centered only on ourselves will develop into greed. The exercise of freedom without the divine law generates permissiveness and licentiousness. The wrong use of love becomes lust. When we do not live centered on God our natural pride of being a child of God becomes vanity and arrogance. If not used properly to help others, our talents and creativity are often turned into maliciousness.

Kallistos Ware, a Greek Orthodox Bishop expressed with eloquence: *"An essential aspect of guarding the heart is warfare against the passions. By passion is meant any disordered appetite or longing that violently takes possession of the soul: anger, jealousy, gluttony, avarice, lust, pride and the rest. Our aim is not to eliminate the passions but to redirect their energy. Uncontrolled rage must be turned into righteous indignation, spiteful jealousy into zeal for the truth, sexual lust into an eros that is pure in its fervor. The passions then are to be purified, not killed; to be educated, not eradicated; to be used positively, not negatively. We say not suppress, but transfigure."*

There is not one basic desire or element in the human character that is essentially evil. **Good and evil are a matter of direction.** When our original desires are misdirected, it results in our "fallen nature", basically selfishness. For this reason, the root of our wrong conduct is the reversal of the main forces for goodness.

According to the *Divine Principle* we have two purposes: The purpose for the whole that directs us to live unselfishly for others and the individual purpose that urges us to pursue our own well-being. We were created with a good original nature that maintains those two purposes in harmony. However, as a result of the fall, our desires tend to go in a selfish direction generating what we call the "fallen nature". Fallen nature pushes us to put priority on the individual purpose rather than the purpose for the whole. Selfishness is so common that we almost do not recognize it.

Selfishness does not refer to the natural desire of self-improvement that each person has. We have a natural ambition to ensure our well-being and a desire to reach the highest values. This is not selfishness. These are qualities of our original nature, given by God. Selfishness refers to the erroneous and misdirected use of our desires and ambitions. This misdirection results in greed, envy and vanity, the actions that constitute poison for our spiritual life.

Selfishness is a perversion of our original nature. Life presents to us an endless series of choices, and by being blind towards spiritual reality we make erroneous decisions.

Selfishness can be compared with the attitude of a person who, without enough information, decides to purchase something in the market. Later, having received more information, it is realized that an incorrect decision was made. Similarly, those who live a selfish life while on earth will feel frustrated after they die, realizing their wrong decisions.

We have the desire to do what is good but, we do not do it. Instead, we do evil that we do not desire. From these conflicts inside ourselves appear the conflicts in the world. We can compare man to a cup with a hole in it. The purpose of the cup is to contain liquid, but the liquid flows out at the other end. It is essential to seal that hole by overcoming and eliminating our fallen nature which continues to multiply through the misuse of love.

Having caused the fall, Satan extended his power and strengthened his control over humanity. Although Satan was the cause of this situation, he has been accusing men and women of violating the heavenly law, starting with our first ancestors. Satan's goal has always been to separate us from God and keep us in spiritual ignorance regarding our true value and position as God's children.

Satan does this in two ways. Firstly, he constantly accuses us of disobeying the commandments and laws of our Creator. Secondly, he tempts and seduces us to act in such a way that we prove that his accusations are valid. Satan manipulates our vulnerability to sin. He exploits our weakness, ambition, pride, passion and egocentricity. While we think we are expressing our own desires, we are actually simply doing what Satan really wants us to do. We are not mere slaves of an alien master but are his willing subjects. His influence is entirely spiritual. Because our spiritual perception deteriorated, we do not easily recognize Satan's negative influence.

Like a powerful invisible mafia boss whose illegal activities are done through other people, Satan never appears to us openly. He works anonymously and incognito. Satan works through our own "fallen nature".

We can recognize four fundamental tendencies in our "fallen nature":

1. Our inability to love and see from God's point of view, resulting in a selfish attitude.

The main reason for the archangel's fall was his inability to love Adam and Eve from God's point of view. Instead, he took his own direction and developed envy and jealousy towards them.

We find selfishness at the core of fallen nature. It is characterized by the tendency of always taking a critical attitude towards others, focusing on our partial and self-centered viewpoint.

Instead of appreciating others we try to compare ourselves with them and develop envy and jealousy. Students may feel jealous of other students who seem to be the favorite of the teacher. In the workplace people may feel jealous of their colleagues who are promoted because of their excellent work. Instead of finding value in others, we are very often rather delighted to find something bad in others so as to make us appear and feel better.

The failure to see things from God's point of view, moves us gradually away from the truth and leads us, step by step, to believe in the untrue, to distrust everyone, to be judgmental and have a rebellious attitude. The first error of Adam and Eve was not to believe the words of God, and instead believe the false words of the archangel, which finally drove them to disobey God's commandment.

2. Abandoning our position of responsibility.

The archangel did not appreciate the value of his position given by God. Instead of finding satisfaction in fulfilling his responsibility, he hoped to find it in taking the role of Adam and in even usurping God's own position.

Similarly, it is very easy for us to abandon our position of responsibility. We escape from our responsibilities to search for the easy way out. When something goes wrong we complain. We have the tendency to accuse and blame others for our own errors or misfortunes.

The most serious consequence of this fallen nature is the desire for a complete experience of love before we are mature in heart. There is a tendency of using others to experience momentary sexual pleasure. The sin of fornication and adultery is always related to an abandoning of our own position.

3. The reversal of dominion or order of authority.

Human beings were supposed to be the natural leaders of the archangel. Lucifer, however, refused to submit to Adam and Eve but tyrannized them instead. Without the qualification of heart, he could only become a false leader maintaining control through deceit, lies and fear.

Like Lucifer, fallen people often become arrogant and do not follow the person who is better qualified than ourselves. Instead of influencing others with love and truth, we try to take control of others by means of force and deception. This is the root of exploitation.

One of the most serious aspects of fallen nature is the tendency to try to dominate others.

We think that we are better than others because of our position, intelligence, race or nationality. Another example of this reversal of dominion, as already mentioned, is the dominion of our carnal desire over our conscience.

Because of fallen nature, leaders are trying to get power through methods such as coercion, force and deceit. The twentieth century has witnessed big examples of this problem. Because of our bad experience with leaders, we tend to distrust anyone in a position of leadership. Envy, arrogance, hate, aggressiveness, violence and murder are always related to this aspect of fallen nature.

To liberate ourselves from this attitude we must love others truly and unconditionally. We must know how to forgive and serve even our enemies until they are naturally won over by our good heart.

4. The multiplication of evil and the tendency of self-justification.

In the same way as the archangel multiplied or passed false love to Eve and then from Eve to Adam, we also try to pass on our bad habits and wrong behavior to others.

We try to involve others in our wrong conduct. As more and more people accept vice and sin, it seems to be less false. The result of all of this is the loss of absolute values. Everything seems to rely on the view of the majority rather than on principle. The increased social acceptance of immorality seems to make us feel less guilty. Due to the multiplication of evil, we lost the standard of good and evil. Sometimes we are unsure of what is right or wrong and this causes great confusion.

There are two particular consequences to this insensitivity and they allow evil to continue. One is the desperation or lack of hope which leads us to believe that there is no way of transforming this world into a place of goodness. The other is the irresponsibility which makes us believe that evil is only a natural element in our world and will disappear by itself.

It is important to recognize all these elements of our fallen nature so that we can successfully overcome and conquer the wrong within ourselves.

POSSIBLE CRITICISM OF THIS VISION

Having been confronted with this new explanation about the origin of evil and immorality, it is perhaps possible that some readers may feel skeptical. One could ask: who could know all these details of the behavior and motivations of Adam, Eve and the Archangel? Most people probably consider these descriptions as pure fabrication of an ancient myth and doubt the historicity of these events.

This reaction is perfectly natural, especially from the viewpoint of atheists and agnostics. It is also to be expected in the case of people who lack a firm religious belief and doubt the existence of life after death, thus maintaining a materialistic interpretation of the origin of life.

A materialistic, agnostic or radically atheist point of view must not be used, however, as an excuse to reject the valuable moral teachings arise by this interpretation, nor to serve as an rational justification for immorality or wrong behavior. We could therefore speak of two types of atheists. One which insist: "there is not God, neither life after our physical death, so that I can do as I please here in this world." And the other that reasons: "Because God doesn't exist, I have to be responsible for this world and do all those good things that God was suppose to do if He had existed." Those who determine to become this type of responsible atheists, loving and serving others unconditionally and avoid illicit love, very soon will discover the Divine in themselves. The historic root of evil, as we have previously exposed, does not originate in atheism, but rather in a selfish and irresponsible attitude.

For people of faith confronted with this new idea, our advice would be one of caution, prudence and a call for serious reflection in the face of the challenge that new discoveries always bring. It takes a tremendous effort, humility, tolerance and a great mental openness to change our previous concepts or to consider new approaches without committing ourselves to make quick prejudgments until we have done our own in-depth investigations.

Through intense and sincere prayer one could receive answers. Another possible method is through a direct search in the spirit world. Obviously, that is where the best archives and answers will be found. Because there we can find the total and complete records of all past history. There we would find the men and women as well as the angels who played a key role in the events that occurred in the past.

These discoveries are a revelation obtained by Rev. Sun Myung Moon, based on enormous and intense efforts following the above-mentioned methods.

For those who consider the story of Genesis in the Bible as pure mythology, it is very likely that they will perceive these new revelations as fiction.

However, even assuming that all these revelations were interpreted in that way and this message was to be taken as purely symbolic or mythical, we can never dismiss, renounce or forsake the ethical and moral value of what is proclaimed here, as a valuable guide towards virtue, for the following reasons:

1. This approach, without any doubt, offers a powerful affirmation and defense for monogamy in marriage, for the family, for true love and for all the values necessary to maintain a sound society.

2. It introduces an excellent explanation of the fundamental reasons why we should avoid free sex, adultery and infidelity, and provides us with the best possible protection and solutions.

   In the face of the increasing AIDS epidemic which, unfortunately due to the erroneous approaches taken until now, will plunge whole nations into a crisis of catastrophic proportions, we can recognize that only purity and fidelity are the best acceptable antidotes.

3. It reveals to us with clarity and accuracy the reasons and motives why man became separated from God.

4. It warns about the absolute and sacred power of love, as the source of happiness or tragedy.

5. This explanation reveals, psychologically, a great deal about ourselves, our attitudes and tendencies. It is consistent with the well-known patterns of behavior constantly repeated throughout human history.

6. It provides us with a valuable guide and advice to overcome our selfishness and fallen nature.

7. It offers very plausible answers about the historic origin of selfishness, shame, envy, illicit love, immorality, family disintegration and breakdown and all the resulting problems and vices that create human alienation.

There are those of us who will believe in this interpretation and feel inspired and grateful for the benefit that it brings to our spiritual life.

What only remains to be said at this point, is that we sincerely expect from all those who do not share the same opinion that they will accept the challenge to offer a better answer to the questions and problems presented here.

CIRCUMCISION, CELIBACY AND
THE SACRAMENT OF MARRIAGE

The *Divine Principle* coincides with St. Irenaeus in observing that the work of redemption follows exactly the same stages of man's fall. For each false step done by man, seduced by Satan, God demands a compensation, so that our victory over the seducer will be complete.

The knowledge and insight of what really happened in the beginning allow us to understand better certain religious practices such as circumcision, celibacy and the sacrament of marriage.

According to Genesis, Abraham initiated the ceremonial act of circumcision, as a visible sign of the covenant binding the children of Israel to their God. Humans fell by the misuse of the sexual parts and as restitution for that act, the boy's foreskin was cut. Cutting off the skin of the sexual organ could be said to indicate our determination to cut our attachment to Satan and the false sexual love that he taught.

These revelations about the fall have great merit because they show exactly how sin is rooted in man's biological structure.

As we know, the fall occurred through sexual love. For this reason, all the world religions have considered fornication and adultery to be among the worst sins.

In a way, and putting aside some of the details of his theories, Sigmund Freud correctly traced human neurosis to uncontrolled and un-sublimated sexual desire. The early church fathers had already connected the original sin with the sin of concupiscence.

It is meaningful to notice that in many cases these leaders demanded from priests a life of sexual abstinence and celibacy, as a way of purification and sanctity. This permitted the establishing of a good standard and was an example of discipline and self-control to strengthen their followers.

No one could ignore the praise that Jesus Christ and the Apostle Paul gave to the practice of religious celibacy for those very exceptional men and women with the determination to follow this path (Mt. 19:12, I Cor. 7).

Let us examine for a moment the case of Mother Ann Lee Stanley, who officially founded the celibate Shakers. While being imprisoned in 1770 in Manchester, England, she had a vision of Jesus Christ in which he graphically showed her that, in respect to the original sin, the sexual act was the true act of transgression committed by the first man and woman in the Garden of Eden. After this surprising experience, she and her followers settled down in celibate communities in which they lived together as brothers and sisters.

Many of those who have the vocation to live a life of celibacy, in a way, feel intuitively that they should go the way of restoration as brothers and sisters, waiting for the absolute permission from God to establish a sacred and divine marriage, that could only be bestowed at some time in the future. So, they chose to "marry" spiritually with the Lord and His work.

In the process of restoration vertical love has to be upheld and horizontal love must be denied, because human history started with illicit horizontal love. Now we can understand why the most prominent religions always emphasized individual denial. In attempting to deny everything in the human world, religious people led ascetic, isolated lives, searching for the lost vertical original true love, trying to overcome sexual temptations and remain on the side of God. Such emphasis on religious celibacy occurred because they had to resist the temptation of worldly love to reach later the vertical love of God.

This clarifies the inner reason why religions like Hinduism, Buddhism and many forms of Christianity taught that, for those who truly seek the divine, the most straight and sublime path requires sexual abstinence.

In the Catholic Church for example, priests, monks and nuns maintain vows of permanent celibacy as the best spiritual path for their personal salvation, and to minister to other people.

If Jesus Christ did not get married, it is natural that their faithful followers should not be different from their Teacher in that regard.

Under this prospect, marriage was considered by some early church fathers as recommendable and good, but, at the same time, as a secondary or an alternative way for those unable to follow the difficult path of abstinence. On March 25, 1954, Pope Pius XII in his encyclical on Consecrated Virginity reminded us how the Church Fathers have abundantly illustrated the numerous advantages in spiritual growth which result from a complete renouncement of sexual pleasure. It is not to be thought that such pleasure, when it arises from lawful marriage, is reprehensible in itself; on the contrary, the chaste use of marriage is ennobled and sanctified by a special sacrament, as the Fathers themselves have clearly remarked. Nevertheless, it must be equally admitted that as a consequence of the fall of Adam the lower faculties of human nature are no longer obedient to right reason, and may involve man in dishonorable actions. As Thomas Aquinas mentioned, the use of marriage "keeps the soul from full abandon to the service of God."

The council of Trent lauded the excellence of virginity and of celibacy and spoke of their superiority over the married state. Consecrated virginity was preferable to marriage when devoting oneself wholly to the service of God. The heart of married persons will remain more or less "divided" between the love of God and the love of spouse. The Apostle Paul wrote: "But if they cannot exercise self-control, they should marry. For it is better to marry than to be aflame with passion." (1 Cor. 7:9). Even the priests of the Old Testament had to abstain from the marriage act during the period of their service in the temple.

All of this implies a certain admission that the sacrament of marriage has not yet the full blessing and sanctification from God.

Unfortunately, Jesus Christ could leave for posterity only a model of individual perfection. He never married, nor established a real family model, for all his disciples to imitate and follow. The ignorance of the people in recognizing him as the Messiah provoked rejection and subsequent crucifixion, preventing the restoration of a true couple and family, to supplant the false family model inherited from the fall.

The Christian family, as a monogamous and stable couple, was of course the appropriate and natural structure for the children, as well as the best way to avoid immorality and promiscuity. But this does not represent a complete model of the restored ideal family that was lost with the fall. This is demonstrated by the fact that Christian theologians cannot deny that even the most devout Christian couples still transmit the original sin to their descendants.

Until the present time, for the majority of Christian churches the bond of the sacrament of marriage has a temporal and conditional validity: "Until death do us part." However, we all have an eternal and indestructible spirit given by God. In the ideal world that God wants to see established, death only represents the separation from our physical body that decomposes, but that fact in no way separates or divorces us from our spouse, children or people whom we love and with whom we will finally meet in the Spirit World.

With whom are we going to experience and share the intimacy of our being, day by day in an endless forever? Obviously that person will be our spouse and of course such union will include the Spirit of God fusing together with each couple in enjoying the blessed sexual love of such a marriage. Regardless of our love and gratitude for Jesus Christ or other extraordinary men and women, they are not the persons with whom (according to the original purpose of creation) we are destined to fuse together and become two in one flesh.

We cannot see the invisible and intangible God, just as we cannot see our mind (here or in the spiritual world). Our spouse should become the face of God for each of us, and because God has no hands to embrace us, our spouse's embrace and love should be the embrace of God.

Celibacy, as a way to perfection, has been a common practice in Christianity, Buddhism, Hinduism, and other faiths until now because marital love needs to be restored and the ideal of the family has not yet been established at the level that God had originally intended, had the fall never occurred. Once this ideal conjugal love is achieved, this will end the need for celibacy.

In the world where marriage has been properly instituted, happiness will extend from the love of the couple, centering on the sexual act which should have a mystic and sacred dimension, and will result in God-centered families, communities, nations and a world of freedom, peace unification and happiness.

As will be explained later, we are still waiting for the eternal and true blessing of God for the establishment of a heavenly marriage that restores us to our lost original position.

THE ORIGINAL SIN AFFECTS OUR LINEAGE

Love is the origin of life. The false love experienced by our first ancestors transmitted life to their descendants and affected our lineage very deeply.

In the Bible we read a truly astonishing and revealing comment by Jesus Christ: "They [the Pharisees] said to him: 'We are not born of fornication; we have one Father, even God'. Jesus said to them, 'If God were your Father, you would love me, for I proceeded and came forth from God... You are of your father the devil, and your will is to do your father's desires" (Jn. 8:41-48).

Jesus clearly declared that our father is not God, that our father is the Devil, who has been a murderer and liar from the beginning. Is this not a shocking declaration?

Jesus as well as John the Baptist on some occasions referred to people as a "brood of vipers", making allusion to our false lineage (Lk. 3:7, Mt. 12:34 and Mt. 23:33).

Therefore, the original sin is a sin that affects the lineage and has been transferred from generation to generation. We are born of satanic lineage as the descendants of satanic love.

From the moment our life is conceived in the mother's womb, that life indirectly has a connection with the love that Satan instead of God taught in the beginning. Many early church fathers understood that the original sin was transmitted from the first couple to all descendants through the act of sexual love of our progenitors. Figuratively speaking, it is almost as if a kind of spiritual virus has been passed on from generation to generation.

We cannot be blamed personally for what happened in the beginning of our history. Nevertheless, whether we are conscious or ignorant of it, whether we like it or not, the fact remains that we inherited this lineage originated by our first ancestors. All of us, in a way, have to lament as the author of Psalm 51:7. "Behold, I was brought forth in iniquity, and in sin did my mother conceive me".

This tragedy came to the world by the Devil, the fallen archangel, who initiated man's sexual love instead of God. And that is why Jesus Christ called him our father. We have fallen under the satanic sovereignty, because Satan became the false father and the owner of this world.

It is clear by now that the original sin is the sin of the fall and that we received these satanic elements or tendencies from generation to generation. Because of the nature of this crime or original sin, its liquidation has been an extremely difficult task.

The original sin committed by our ancestors is like the contamination of the root of the genealogical tree of humanity.

Starting from that sin, humanity has been constantly violating heavenly law, generating a sinful tradition. The repercussions of these sins by our ancestors are inherited by the descendants for restitution. We also need to consider the collective sins committed by a particular group which later affects the nation, race or even the whole of humanity. Finally we have our own personal sins.

To a limited degree, it is possible to cleanse and restore our personal and inherited sins. We do so through efforts such as admitting faults, repenting, requesting forgiveness and paying compensation. However, to eliminate the original sin, connected to the entire human lineage, is beyond our capacity. This is why, humanity needs a savior.

Only the one who finally discovered what Satan did to the first human couple and their descendants can remove the original sin and restore us again to the divine lineage with the power and the authority of God.

Once our original sin is forgiven and eliminated, it will be much easier to establish a future world free of sin. A world in which each person, with the power and inspiration of God, will be able to overcome evil and where Satan will never be able to operate and accuse man.

The desire for illicit love is deeply ingrained in the human heart. Sexual sin and the sin of illicit love are very difficult to overcome. However, our restoration can never be possible or fulfilled unless each man can withstand the temptation of a naked beautiful woman in the same bed with him.

Jesus Christ requested from us a very high standard of purity:
"You have heard that it was said, 'You shall not commit adultery.' But I say to you that every one who looks at a woman lustfully has already committed adultery with her in his heart." (Mt. 5:27-28).

Immoral acts are always committed secretly and in a free society there is almost no way to prevent them, except to elevate our heart and conscience. Simple laws, punishments or other acceptable external methods, prove, so much now as in the past, to be ineffective to control them. As human beings can not live without experiencing love, if we are not able to live by the laws of true love is evident that the alternative is illicit love.

People should be clearly informed of the terrible consequences that this kind of immoral behavior causes to our eternal life. We have only one life and only one first love or virginity. If we lose our life and die, there is no possibility of bringing someone back to life and the same can be said for our first love.

As William Graham Cole wrote: "Stolen objects can be returned or compensated, lies and defamation can be retracted and corrected, envy and jealousy can be overcome. But a sexual act committed with another person cannot be nullified. The mutual relationship suffers a radical change and the affected couple will never again be the same as before. Something indelible has marked them."

Our virginity, which represents our first and true love, is the most valuable and holy possession that no amount of money can possibly buy. Once it is lost, it is irrecoverable. Once we are aware of this fact, it is a real tragedy to give away such a priceless possession in an idle moment of passion or lust. Such an action can have devastating consequences for those involved, and for their future attitudes and behavior.

Even religious leaders, who inspired many with their faith and carried out great accomplishments, often succumb to such temptations.

There are those who think that these weaknesses are rather natural and part of our intrinsic human nature. They feel that it is useless to try and change ourselves.

However, Jesus Christ clearly pointed out that in the context of love, human perfection is possible: "You, therefore, must be perfect as your heavenly Father is perfect." (Mat. 5:48).

Paradoxically, our path to perfection implies, on the one hand, to grow to and attain true love. It also means living sacrificially for the sake of others, including our enemies, even at the cost of life itself. And, on the other hand, to abstain from loving in the wrong way, avoiding illicit sexual love. In short, **we are called to love from God's viewpoint and refuse the forbidden love.**

The efforts to avoid and overcome these problems that have traditionally been carried out by self-discipline or permanent celibacy are commendable and worthy of admiration. But, unfortunately, they do not represent either a full eradication of sin, nor do they constitute a realistic and complete solution to the problem.

How then, will we finally be able to resolve this difficult situation? It is obvious, that the only antidote or lasting solution would be the experience of true, eternal and unchangeable love within a marriage recognized and blessed by God.

Pure and true love is the irreplaceable medicine to cure both, the lack of love and tainted love. To draw an analogy, when we satisfy ourselves with good food, we automatically abandon the desire for poor quality food or the necessity to fast.

Light drives darkness away and only the authentic love will quiet the desire for any substitute that we may have had.

That is why only the achievement of divine love between man and woman will ensure our success in totally eradicating the desire for ungodly love. This would eliminate infidelity, adultery, divorce, prostitution, rape and other deviations in human conduct.

After 21 years of analyzing this problem, this is my conclusion: **The day that every man and woman understand, already as adolescents, the sacred and fundamental value of true love, and arrive willingly and naturally pure and virgins to their blessing in marriage and thereafter maintain absolute fidelity to their true love partners, a concrete and firm hope will exist to solve all of the other countless human problems, because THIS basic problem, (as the hole in the cup) is the basic and the most difficult to solve.**

Personally, I made a pledge to God to dedicate my life (here or in the spiritual world, working inside or outside any particular organization is not important) to contribute to this goal, because I came to realize the sacred and mystical value of the love between husband and wife together with God and the huge tragedy that results with the destruction or the pollution of such love. Therefore, the act of "the fall" is not just an incident (or a myth for some) that occurred at the dawn of our existence on this planet; but a tragedy that is happening every moment in this world, and this is the way we separate from the divine ideal and kill our relationship with God in ourselves.

To resolve this problem, humanity has to receive new ancestors, who can be substituted for Adam and Eve, the fallen parents. These new ancestors, in the position of True Parents, represent the love of God and God's lineage. They will separate us from the false lineage. They will eliminate the original sin in each man and woman. They will engraft us into the true lineage of God and will transmit to us the blessing to establish a sacred and eternal marriage recognized by God.

True families, living according to heavenly tradition, will multiply, gradually creating a foundation to build the dreamed of and long-awaited utopia of a better world.

In this way, God's and humanity's anxiously desired ideal, lost by the fall, will be restored.

THE REALIZATION OF A WORLD OF TRUE LOVE

As we have revealed in full detail, Adam and Eve separated themselves from God and could not achieve perfection. Therefore God could not bless them in a heavenly marriage and human history started with a satanic instead of a Godly lineage.

It is truly astonishing to realize that, even with so many billions of people having lived on earth, God has never truly had His own family. Not a single family was ever formed with the full and complete blessing of God. We are all descendants of the fallen Adam and Eve. If Adam and Eve would have united with God, they would have established the marriage of the Lamb mention in the Bible. God Himself would also have been married that same day, with the same joy, the same fulfillment, accomplishing in this way the whole purpose of creation. It is truly heartwarming to realize that, throughout the thousands of years of history, God's total goal has been the restoration of mankind into His own family. He has been longing for the day that the first heavenly wedding ceremony could take place, a divine marriage between a perfect man and woman.

God wanted to see this heavenly marriage during the time of Jesus Christ. Jesus came as the Messiah, God's only begotten Son, the first man on earth without sin. He came to earth as the second Adam (1 Cor. 15:45). He was supposed to be the first perfect bridegroom on earth. As the culmination of his ministry, Jesus Christ should have restored a heavenly bride, fulfilling the prophecy of the "marriage of the Lamb." Together with his Bride, Jesus should have been installed as the True Parents of mankind, establishing the first family of God on earth.

The faithlessness of the people of that time, however, did not allow this glorious day to come in Jesus Christ's time. On the contrary, he was rejected and crucified. Ever since that time, humanity was destined to receive another Adam who would establish the position of "True Parents", in the place of the first fallen parents.

Unificationists believe that at this time Rev. Sun Myung Moon has successfully completed the messianic mission that Jesus Christ entrusted to him in his youth. In spite of indescribable tribulations, persecution and opposition, he was finally victorious, not only in deciphering the hidden secret of the root of the original sin, but also in finding a true solution to overcome and remove it.

In 1960, after fulfilling all the required conditions and following God's command, Sun Myung Moon and his wife Hak Ja Han received this heavenly blessing to recreate the pure and sinless marriage that was lost since the time of the fall. They were subsequently further blessed by God with fourteen children. This marriage is considered by Unificationists as the foundation and starting point for God's future blessings to all mankind.

That is why, since 1960, Rev. and Mrs. Moon blessed in holy matrimony successively larger numbers of couples at weddings within the Unification Movement. In 1960, 36 couples, and in later years 72, 124, 430, 777, 1,800, 8,000 couples and others. The latest one of these memorable ceremonies was held on 25th August 1992, in Seoul, Korea for 30,000 couples, symbolizing a God-centered unity, not just of men and women of all races, but also of numerous different nationalities, coming from all over the world to freely, joyfully and gratefully accept this greatest blessing of all time from our Heavenly Father. This was truly an historical occasion !

The previous day to this large wedding ceremony, on August 24, 1992, before a large international audience of religious and political leaders, scientists, academics and journalists, gathered in Seoul, Korea, Sun Myung Moon announce that he and his wife Hak Ja Han had been chosen by God to be the True Parents and had successfully accomplished their mission. Through the victory of True Parents, this extraordinary marriage blessing is offered to couples from every race, religion and nation on earth, bringing them new meaning and a new standard of family life, and realizing a purification of lineage that offers future generations the real prospect of a completely different and good world. In the future, as people come to understand the value and quality of these precious families, millions will seek such marriages. Through them, God can restore the family that Satan has destroyed. Such restored, God-centered families are the very building blocks of an ideal nation and world.

It is lamentable, that due to the initial rejection by certain Christian leaders of Rev. Moon, an enormous barrier was established that blocked the rapid spread of his important revelation on the fertile ground prepared by Christianity over the last 2,000 years.

It is paradoxical and lamentable that because of this, the most prepared people, pastors, priests, monks and nuns, who should have been the first to receive this great divine blessing, were often the first to oppose these revelations and to think them scandalous.

The Jesuit sociologist Joseph Fichter, who carefully studied the life style and particularly marriage within the Unification Movement, says that Unificationists "have found a family program that works. While marriage counselors and priests in parishes put their hands to their head not knowing what to do about the breakdown of family life, the Unification Church is doing something about it. The family centered on God is not merely a nice slogan or a spiritual ideal suggested by the leaders of the Church. It is the fundamental essence of the communion between the faithful of the Church."

"One has to recognize their systematic program for the restoration of the "old fashioned" morality, their emphasis on chastity before marriage, prayers in preparation for marriage, readiness to accept guidance in the selection of the couple, marital love as a reflection of the love of God, and the transmission of spiritual perfection to their children. There have been many comments and much criticism of the theological, political and economic aspects of the Unification Movement, but very little has been said about the positive and valuable implications in regard to marriage and family."

Due to this initial rejection of many Christian leaders, Rev. Sun Myung Moon, very heartbroken because of this situation, had to begin practically from zero and was obliged, contrary to his wishes, to create his own religious organization.

Professor Young Oon Kim, doctor in theology and one of the few Christian leaders in Korea who recognized the value of this message from the beginning, commented in one of her speeches:

"Rev. Moon organized the Unification Church in Korea in 1954. From the beginning, he told us that we are not a denominational movement, the Church is not our goal, nor the axis in order to create the Kingdom of Heaven. It is merely the instrument to teach the *Divine Principle*, elevate the members spiritually and carry on the work of God. When we reach our goal, the Church will be dissolved".

What is then that goal? Rev. Moon exposed it with clarity in a sermon on September 11, 1974:

"What is our purpose? To become true men and women. We will create the true husband and wife and become true parents to give birth to children who experience love among themselves and form a loving brotherhood. And those children and parents together will create one heavenly family. The family will expand into a true society. That true society will expand into a true nation. That true nation will expand into a true world."

Rev. Moon has founded literally hundreds of organizations in the academic, scientific, economic and political fields, in the area of mass media, humanitarian projects, etc., with the purpose of bringing this world closer to God and to create a base of genuine trust, credibility and recognition so that these revelations could at last be understood and accepted by humanity. But finally the central and fundamental mission of Rev. Moon is to give this original blessing from God to create true couples and true families.

Rev. Sun Myung Moon has now the permission and authority from God to transmit this "blessing" which allows us to eliminate original sin completely, to separate from the fallen lineage and to be engrafted in the lineage of God.

THE WAY TOWARDS WORLD PEACE

**A COMMON FATHER - GOD - ONE IDEOLOGY CENTRED ON GOD
UNITY BETWEEN CHRISTIANITY AND ALL WORLD RELIGIONS
INTERNATIONAL AND INTERRACIAL MARRIAGES
A COMMUNITY OF NATIONS, PEOPLES AND RACES
HARMONY BETWEEN RELIGION AND SCIENCE
UNITY OF EAST AND WEST, NORTH AND SOUTH**

DIAGRAM 8

To conclude this essay, I would like to quote the message given by Reverend and Mrs. Moon to the 2075 couples who participated in the wedding ceremony performed on July 1

1982, at the Madison Square Garden stadium, New York, in which the author had the privilege to participate:

"The establishment of happy, righteous families as the source of life, love and joy, has been the goal of God and man throughout history. To realize this ideal, each one of you has dedicated months and years of preparation, often under very difficult circumstances. We can all be justly proud to meet here together on this day, to add another great building block to the Kingdom of Heaven on Earth.

"Until today, the eyes of the world have been upon our church; after today the eyes of the world will be upon you and your families. Remember three things above all in your life together:

1. ***The eternal union between husband and wife.***
   Your marriage is not merely "until death do us part," but for all time eternal. Each spouse is a great key to ever expand and deepen our understanding of the infinite God. In your marriage, God's love is consummated and together you are able to receive His total love.

2. ***The tradition of family love.***
   After seeking ideal marriages, it is your responsibility to educate your children with a commitment to moral excellence. Before you can freely invest your love and energy in other dimensions, you must by all means fulfil your responsibilities as a loving parent.

3. ***The ideal World.***
   Heaven is a world of heart, where all may trust and unite with one another in love. But there will be no true heaven for anyone while people are still in

want, in need or in pain - physically or spiritually. You must all accept your responsibility to work as world citizens so that the legacy you leave to your children and grandchildren will be the harmonized world of God's love.

"God bless you in all that you undertake and may He give you the vision and strength you need to realize His Kingdom on earth. That is the task facing us all."

Hallelujah!, For the Lord our God the Almighty reigns. Let us rejoice and exult and give him the glory, for the marriage of the Lamb has come, and his Bride has made herself ready... Blessed are those who are invited to the marriage supper of the Lamb... (Rev. 19:6-9).

BIBLIOGRAPHY

In the realization of this essay the following books were consulted:

- Divine Principle, (HSA-UWC)
- Outline of The Principle level 4
- Divine Principle. Study Guide, Young Whi Kim
- Unification Theology & Christian Thought, Young Oon Kim
- Unification Theology, Young Oon Kim
- Presentations on the Unification Principle, (CARP)
- International Leadership Seminar, Outline of Presentations, (CARP)
- Divine Principle Home Study Course, (HSA-UWC)
- God's Warning to The World I, II, Rev. Sun Myung Moon, (HSA-UWC)
- God's Will and The World, Rev. Sun Myung Moon, (HSA-UWC)
- The Path of a Pioneer (HSA Publications)
- A Prophet Speaks Today, The Words of Sun Myung Moon, (HSA-UWC)
- The Way of Tradition Vol. I, II, III, IV, (HSA-UWC)
- Rev. Sun Myung Moon, Public Talks Vol. I (U.F.E. Publications)
- Guidance for Heavenly Tradition, Young Whi Kim
- Pecado, sexo y autocontrol, Norman Vincent Peale (Editorial Grijalbo)
- Fundamentals of Unification Thought, Sang Hun Lee (U.T.I.)
- True Love, Reverend Sun Myung Moon. Vol. One, (HSA-UWC)

- And the publications: Unification News (HSA-UWC)
    Today's World (HSA-UWC)
    Blessing Quarterly (HSA-UWC)

This essay, although it makes references to the teachings of Rev. Sun Myung Moon and the Unification Church, does not represent and should not be considered an official publication of the Unification Movement. The full responsibility for the contents of this work rests solely on its author.

For more information or correspondence with the author, please write to:

Jesus Gonzalez Losada
jesus.gonzalez.losada@gmail.com